Integrating Children's Literature in the Curriculum

Integrating Children's Literature in the Curriculum

Insights for the Primary and Early Years Educator

Rosemary Waugh and David Waugh

Open University Press

Open University Press
McGraw Hill
8th Floor, 338 Euston Road
London
England
NW1 3BH

email: enquiries@openup.co.uk
world wide web: www.openup.co.uk

First edition published 2022

A catalogue record of this book is available from the British Library

Executive Editor: Eleanor Christie
Editorial Assistant: Zoe Osman
Content Product Manager: Ali Davis

ISBN-13: 9780335250806
ISBN-10: 0335250807
eISBN: 9780335250813

Library of Congress Cataloging-in-Publication Data
CIP data applied for

Typeset by Transforma Pvt. Ltd., Chennai, India

Praise page

"This energising and highly practical book offers teachers clear evidence of the power and potential of children's literature. Underpinned by research evidence and examples from classroom practice, this is an informed and supportive guide for teachers and student teachers alike. Read on to enrich your practice right across the curriculum and find diverse books to engage and inspire children. Enjoy!"

Professor Teresa Cremin, The Open University, UK

"How do we make sure children today recognise the value of reading for pleasure when so many other mediums are competing for their attention? The answer lies within this excellent text. Throughout the book the authors explore the essential role of creating a culturally rich environment for all children from a young age, using classic fiction and newfound literature. Poetry and rhyme are used to demonstrate how all children should be represented and included in the texts they learn to read and understand. Developing empathy is explored; children take deep dives into works and extend their own vocabulary when investigating language and presenting such to their peers. Examples of how children can become writers of their own literature are interwoven with the clear message that through excellent modelling and witnessing their teacher's love of reading will the next generation become passionate about literature in the world around them."

Megan Stephenson, PGCE Primary ITT Lead,
Leeds Trinity University, UK

"**Integrating Children's Literature in the Curriculum** *by David Waugh and Rosemary Waugh is a highly recommended book for student teachers and for teachers with vast experience in the classroom. Cultural and ethnic diversity is explored deeply, and inclusion of all pupils is at the very heart of this book. The book makes children's literature accessible to all through a huge range of texts used in case studies which are backed up by up-to-date research including an analysis of the effects on reading and writing after the lockdowns. It is an essential book for the primary school – needed now more than ever before."*

Adam Bushnell, Author of Modelling Exciting Writing
and Descriptosaurus: Story Writing

Contents

Acknowledgements

We are grateful to everyone who granted permission for their work to be quoted in this book. We are particularly grateful to Karen Robertson, Assistant Headteacher at Holbeach Primary School in Catford, South East London, for sharing her school's excellent practice and for producing two case studies for us. Paige Brown, a trainee teacher at the University of Worcester, who now teaches at Ledbury Primary School, provided inspirational insights into the virtual classroom she set up while on school placement during lockdown.

Thanks to all of the teachers and trainee teachers who inspired the case studies in this book. Their exemplary practice offers considerable hope for the future.

Finally, thanks to all the wonderful authors and poets, past and present, who have given us so much inspiration and continue to open new worlds for readers.

Foreword

Children's literature matters

Stories spark our imaginations, fire our emotions, help us solve problems and develop empathy. The themes and topics of literature, which are as broad as the world itself, provide rich opportunities for connections to be made – connections between our own lives and the text, between the text and the world, and between the text and other texts. In addition, and significantly, through sharing children's literature, young people are enabled to make interpersonal connections with one another, with their families and with their teachers. Through sharing 'books in common' they develop a sense of belonging and a richer understanding of others' values, morals and perspectives as well as their own (Cremin et al., 2014).

However, education policies and national curricula tend to take children's literature for granted. At the primary phase, its potency is rarely really recognised by politicians; it is often simply assumed to be a tool to teach reading and a stimulus for comprehension and writing. Only some of it is deemed to be culturally rich enough material for children's leisurely enjoyment.

Teachers know better. They recognise that the quality and diversity of the texts that they read aloud to their classes, that they delve into in English and across the curriculum and those that they recommend for voluntary reading make a difference. Teachers know that narrative matters, that literature in all its forms and formats can tempt and delight even the most reluctant reader. They know that powerful stories engage youngsters, both cognitively and affectively.

Researchers know this too; the evidence is unequivocal. The psychologist Jerome Bruner (1986) and the linguist Barbara Hardy (1977) are among myriad scholars who have shown that as humans we make sense of the world through story, that literature renders the world less fixed and more susceptible to re-consideration and re-creation. Researchers also reveal the presence of a 'fiction effect' and demonstrate that those teenagers who read fiction books frequently, possess markedly stronger reading skills and attain far higher scores in comprehension tests than their peers who read other genres (Jerrim and Moss, 2018). The role of fictional reading needs to be recognised more fully for its beneficial contribution to academic achievement and to social and emotional development.

Children's authors, too, attest to the power of fiction and poetry. As Katherine Rundell notes in her book entitled *Why You Should Read Children's Books, Even Though You Are So Old and Wise*:

> It is to children's fiction that you turn if you want to feel awe and hunger and longing for justice: to make the old warhorse heart stamp again in its stall. (Rundell, 2019: 39)

Her words remind us of the influence of affective and interactive engagement in literature. Affect drives and guides us into reciprocal relationships with texts and their authors, illustrators and designers, and enables us to connect to our own identities as readers – to who we have been, to who we are and who we may become.

Teachers, like researchers and authors, recognise that literature is 'a means by which to think, not a medium through which we are told what to think' (Cliff-Hodges, 2010: 65). They also know that literature is a source of deep satisfaction, mind expansion and pleasure. So, I urge you to read on through this book, learn how to leverage the potential of contemporary and classic children's literature that entices, engages and enables learning right across the curriculum. You will find a great deal to support your journey as Reading Teachers – teachers who read and readers who teach and who reflect on their own reading identities in order to support younger learners.

As you know, children's literature matters. Read on.

Teresa Cremin
Professor of Education, the Open University

References

Bruner, J. (1986) *Actual Minds, Possible Worlds*. Cambridge, MA: Harvard University Press.

Cliff-Hodges, G. (2010) Rivers of reading: Using critical incident collages to learn about adolescent readers and their readership, *English in Education*, 44 (3): 180–199.

Cremin, T., Mottram, M., Powell, S., Collins, R. and Safford, K. (2014) *Building Communities of Engaged Readers: Reading for Pleasure*. London: Routledge.

Hardy, B. (1977) Towards a poetics of fiction: An approach through narrative, in M. Meek, A. Warlow and G. Barton (eds.) *The Cool Web*. London: Bodley Head.

Jerrim, J. and Moss, G. (2018) The link between fiction and teenagers' reading skills: International evidence from the OECD PISA study, *British Educational Research Journal*, 45 (1): 161–181.

Rundell, K. (2019) *Why You Should Read Children's Books, Even Though You Are So Old and Wise*. London: Bloomsbury.

Introduction

Theodor Seuss Geisel, better known as Dr Seuss, the author of more than sixty children's books, stated: "The more that you read, the more things you will know. The more you learn, the more places you'll go" (Dr. Seuss, 1978, p.35). This book invites you to consider ways in which children's literature can be integrated into the curriculum. In it, we will argue that incorporating fiction and poetry into our teaching adds extra dimensions to our exploration of the world around us. Not only does wide engagement with literature help improve our vocabularies and appreciation of language and possibilities, but it also broadens our knowledge of how other people, even fictional characters, live and think. It provides stimuli for discussing issues, including moral dilemmas, and encourages talk about the problems met by characters, which might resonate with children's own experiences but which they might not otherwise discuss. Through literature we can gain added perspective on life in other countries and cultures, as well as on historical events and everyday life in the past.

Throughout the book we have included case studies which illustrate how teachers have developed good practice in integrating children's literature in the curriculum. Each chapter also includes examples of research into reading, as well as activities for you to try as you develop your own practice. At the end of each chapter we provide questions for discussion at staff meetings, seminars and professional development workshops, as well as suggested further reading. You will also find a *For Your Bookshelf* section with some ideas for stories and poems you might like to have in your classroom.

In Chapter 1, we explore reading as an intrinsically pleasurable activity. With so many attractions competing for children's attention, how can we ensure that reading is not only a priority, but also something they engage in because they enjoy it? We cannot just assume that children will engage with literature: we need to make reading appealing and fulfilling. We argue that there are lots of ways teachers and other adults can do this, including by showing that we, too, gain intrinsic pleasure from reading.

Chapter 2 focuses on creating an environment in which reading can flourish. We examine strategies for reading with children, as well as ways of developing the physical environment in order to foster a literature culture. The chapter includes case studies written for us by the literacy coordinator of a school in South London.

Chapter 3 examines ways in which children's literature can enhance and augment teaching and learning across the curriculum. Examples of fiction and poetry being starting points for study are provided, together with suggestions for children's literature which can add depth and interest to different subject studies.

Chapter 4 starts to consider the topic of diversity and inclusion. For example, we look at books in which characters are faced with a range of physical disabilities, learning conditions such as autism, and gender identity issues. Children are often very ready to spot and react to any ways in which people are different; we suggest a range of books which may help children to understand and accept those who are not like themselves or who see the world in a different way.

In Chapter 5, the topic of diversity is continued as we look at issues of race, in the context of an increasingly multi-racial environment. We look at books which show and explain the experiences of immigrant families, and suggest ways in which we can help children to understand the situation of asylum seekers and refugees. We introduce some ideas for books which can help speakers of other languages to make progress in English and to feel less alienated in their new environment.

The theme for Chapter 6 is 'reluctant readers'. We realise that not every child is going to happily settle down with a traditional text book, and look at alternatives such as e-books, graphic novels and picture books, Through other media we can help children who aren't enthusiastic about reading to appreciate that it can be enjoyable.

In Chapter 7, we discuss the concept of classic children's literature and the place of well-established texts in schools. We look at the benefits and the problems in introducing some nineteenth- and twentieth-century books, and consider ways to deal in the classroom with ideas which are no longer 'received wisdom'.

Chapter 8 looks at the value and importance of poetry in the classroom. Both classic and new poems are discussed and, through classroom case studies, some ideas on presentation and performance of poetry are offered. The ways in which vocabulary can be expanded and the phonics of rhyme are considered, along with ideas for looking at the world in different ways through reading poetry, and ideas for creating poetry in the school.

Finally, Chapter 9 provides ideas and guidance for creating children's literature with and for children. We look at examples of novels written with children, as well as at strategies for smaller scale projects which offer opportunities for children to develop their writing and their appreciation of the writing process.

Reading for pleasure is a constant theme throughout the book, and we emphasise the importance of teachers' own knowledge of children's literature and engagement with it. We firmly believe that teachers can have a profound influence on children's reading behaviours and attitudes to literature. By bringing children's literature to the fore in the classroom to enhance learning across the curriculum, we elevate its status and draw upon its many qualities to develop a richer approach to teaching and learning.

Reference

Dr. Seuss (2003) *I Can Read With My Eyes Shut!*. London: HarperCollins Children's Books.

Children's literature as an intrinsic pleasure

Learning outcomes

After reading this chapter, you will have considered:

- The importance of making reading a pleasurable activity for children
- How teachers can introduce children to texts which they might not be able to read independently
- The value of stories and some simple ways of engaging children's interest in them

Link to the Teachers' Standards

3. Demonstrate good subject and curriculum knowledge

- demonstrate an understanding of and take responsibility for promoting high standards of literacy, articulacy and the correct use of standard English

4. Plan and teach well structured lessons

- promote a love of learning and children's intellectual curiosity
- contribute to the design and provision of an engaging curriculum

(DfE, 2011: 11)

Link to the National Curriculum

6.3 Teachers should develop pupils' reading and writing in all subjects to support their acquisition of knowledge. Pupils should be taught to read fluently, understand extended prose (both fiction and non-fiction) and be encouraged to read for pleasure. Schools should do everything to promote wider reading. They should provide library facilities and set ambitious expectations for reading at home.

(DfE, 2013: 10)

Pupils should be taught to:

- develop pleasure in reading, motivation to read, vocabulary and understanding by:
  - listening to and discussing a wide range of poems, stories and non-fiction at a level beyond that at which they can read independently
  - being encouraged to link what they read or hear read to their own experiences
  - becoming very familiar with key stories, fairy stories and traditional tales, retelling them and considering their particular characteristics
  - recognising and joining in with predictable phrases
  - learning to appreciate rhymes and poems, and to recite some by heart
  - discussing word meanings, linking new meanings to those already known

(Year 1 Programme of Study, DfE, 2013: 21)

How often have you heard busy adults say things like, 'When we go on holiday I'm just going to lie beside the pool and read', or 'I just want to curl up with a good book', or even, 'When I retire, I'm going to read all those books I never had time to read'? For many of us, reading is life-enhancing and something to be looked forward to, but for others it is a last resort to fill in time when bored. For children, too, reading can be a pleasure or a chore. We might ask, 'Does it matter if some people don't find reading intrinsically pleasurable?' After all, some people like football and others prefer ballet or rugby union. Shouldn't we just accept that we have different preferences? Surely, providing people can read sufficiently well to do their jobs and manage their finances, etc., it doesn't matter whether they enjoy reading or not. For adults, this may be true, but in this chapter we will argue that, for children developing their reading skills and engaging with the broader curriculum, it is important that we do all we can to enable them to engage with and find intrinsic pleasure in reading.

The importance of developing a love of reading is made clear in the English National Curriculum, which states that 'the overarching aim for English in the national curriculum is to promote high standards of language and literacy by equipping pupils with a strong command of the spoken and written word, and to develop their love of literature through widespread reading for enjoyment' (DfE, 2013: 13).

> The footballer Marcus Rashford, who has helped launch a book club to promote reading, stated: "I wish I was offered the opportunity to really engage with reading more as a child. There were times where the escapism of reading could have really helped me. I want this escapism for all children."
>
> (Marcus Rashford, BBC News, 17.11.20)

A report prepared in the UK by the All-Party Parliamentary Group for Education contended:

> The active encouragement of reading for pleasure should be a core part of every child's curriculum entitlement because extensive reading and exposure to a wide range of texts make a huge contribution to students' educational achievement.
>
> (APPG, 2011: 6)

There is, then, a recognition by government that reading for pleasure is important, so why is it necessary for a famous footballer to devote time and energy to promoting it?

It is all too easy for us, as teachers, to concentrate on the demands of the curriculum for achieving standards of literacy in our classes and overlook those little words 'for pleasure' and 'for enjoyment'. The writer Lucy Mangan, in her memoir of childhood reading, describes watching her small son learning the pleasure of books:

> I can practically see the stream of glittering words flowing into his mind, teaching him in some fundamental way that nothing else can manage how words fit together, how sentences work, how language can be bent this way and that to conjure worlds, feelings, arguments, everything.
>
> (Mangan, 2018: 204)

She describes vividly the excitement of seeing literacy alight in him, and wanting to share the pleasure: 'I want to find a way to grab it in my hands and join the book in stuffing more of it into him' (Mangan, 2018: 204). While of course we will always be concerned with promoting what we might call the mechanics of literacy, we should never lose sight of the passion and excitement of finding new worlds in books, the sharing of experiences and thoughts we may never have met in our everyday lives. For a child to discover a world, whether it's down a rabbit-hole, through a wardrobe, under the floorboards or high in the mountains, a world that will always be there to be visited each time the covers are opened, is a wonderful thing, and this book is about helping you to enable every child to share that experience.

Is there a problem?

One late night in 2003, queues stretched along Oxford Street in London as children and adults sought to buy the next book in J.K. Rowling's Harry Potter series: *Harry Potter and the Order of the Phoenix*. Our oldest granddaughter, then 6, acquired the book on its first day of publication and even though she could not read some of the words, devoured it from cover to cover in one day. It seemed that children's literature had never been so popular. For many children, Harry Potter awakened an enthusiasm for reading, while for others it provided an opportunity to stretch both their ability to decode to aid their comprehension skills, and to engage with a range of concepts. The Potter series became the best-selling children's books of all time, surpassing those of Roald Dahl and Enid Blyton. Despite the success of authors such as Michael Morpurgo, Philip Pullman, Jeff Kinney, R.L. Stine and David Walliams, nothing has approached the same level of popularity since. There is no doubt that many children continue to love reading, but there are some worrying trends which we should be aware of and which are described in the section below.

Research focus: Declining levels of enjoyment

In their 2019 report, the National Literacy Trust (NLT) reported a continued decline in children and young people's levels of reading enjoyment and daily reading. Daily reading was at its lowest level since NLT began reporting it in 2005. Reading enjoyment had 'particularly decreased for boys, children aged 9 to 11, and those who don't receive free school meals' (Clark and Teravainen-Goff, 2020: 14).

The report involved 56,906 children and young people aged 9 to 18 in the UK who were surveyed between January and March 2019. For the first time, 3,748 children aged 5 to 8 completed a survey.

The report explored:

- How many children and young people enjoy reading
- How often they read in their free time
- The type of formats they read, in print and on screens
- How good a reader they think they are
- What they think about reading
- Which groups of young people are more likely to engage in reading
- How reading differs by geographical region

Key findings include:

- Children and young people's levels of reading enjoyment continue to decline and are at their lowest since 2013 (53 per cent said they enjoyed reading in 2019 vs. 53.3 per cent in 2013)
- Children and young people's daily reading levels are the lowest recorded, with just 25.8 per cent of children saying they read daily in their free time in 2019
- Based on reading skills data for 712 pupils aged 11 to 14, young people who enjoy reading are three times more likely to read above the level expected for their age than children who don't enjoy reading (30.1 per cent vs. 8.1 per cent)
- Based on reading skills data for 712 pupils aged 11 to 14, young people who read daily in their free time are twice as likely to read above the level expected for their age than children who don't read daily (37.6 per cent vs. 14.2 per cent)

(NLT survey: Children and young people's reading in 2019 | National Literacy Trust© National Literacy Trust 2020)

The NLT findings are far from isolated, given that the 2016 PIRLS international survey found that in English-speaking countries, apart from Australia, England had the lowest ranking for enjoyment and the lowest for pupil engagement in reading (McGrane et al., 2017). Such findings have caused concern for governments and have influenced the developments to the curriculum. It is recognised that children not only need to learn how to read, but also find pleasure in reading. As Cremin maintained: 'There is no question that the will to read influences the skill and vice versa. Hardly surprising, but it seems to have been enough, alongside concerted campaigning by literacy organisations, to influence policy and now practice' (2019: 5).

Cremin notes Philip Pullman's comment in 1998 that the National Literacy Strategy, which had just been introduced, included more than 55 verbs related to reading, but that 'enjoy' was not one of them. However, Cremin cautions that the emphasis on reading for pleasure in the 2013 curriculum may have led to 'empty demonstrations' designed to show governors, parents, inspectors and children that reading is valued. She states that, 'Many have refurbished or reclaimed their libraries, and some have even purchased double-decker buses, tents, sheds, tree houses and caravans to deck out, as well as cushions, carpets and sofas to enrich classroom reading areas' (Cremin, 2019: 5), but questions whether such initiatives are sufficient.

Certainly, the 2021 Reading Framework recognises the value of children engaging with literature:

> Literature is probably the most powerful medium through which children have a chance to inhabit the lives of those who are like them. All children need to imagine themselves as the main protagonist in a story: celebrating a birthday, going shopping, being ill, having a tantrum, having their hair cut, worrying about a new sibling, being the superhero, going camping, visiting the seaside and having adventures.
>
> (DfE, 2021: 28)

Can we teach children to read for pleasure?

As Cremin states: 'We cannot demand they find pleasure in texts, but we can entice and engage them as readers, and create relaxed invitational spaces in which book talk is valued' (2021: 13). The Reading for Pleasure website is a rich source of practical ideas, provided by practising teachers, which show how initiatives to nurture an enjoyment of reading have worked in their schools. Many of these involve taking what Cremin describes as 'a broadly social view of being a reader' (2021: 13), with children encouraged to discuss the books they read and share recommendations. One example involved a Year 6 teacher creating a secret book club which involved placing a book she had read in a plain brown envelope along with a message on a Post-it that instructed a child whom the teacher knew to be an enthusiastic reader, to read it, and then pass it on to someone else. The book was passed on further, and eventually around ten children became enthusiastic advocates of reading for pleasure. They went on to plant books on unsuspecting pupils' chairs with invitations to read and pass on, and they also created a book display in the school hall. At the heart of this initiative was the teacher's own knowledge of children's literature, something which the Teachers as Readers project sought to address and develop.

Research focus: Teachers as Readers (TaRs)

The Teachers as Readers (TaRs) initiative identified four key elements of pedagogy:

- Reading aloud
- Informal book-talk
- Recommendations
- Independent reading time in a highly social environment

It was found that when teachers had a good knowledge of children's literature and their pupils' reading, the practices 'positively influenced children's attitudes and attainment'.

It concluded that the Reading for Pleasure (RfP) pedagogy enabled teachers to:

- Take responsibility for and plan to develop children's RfP alongside and as complementary to reading instruction
- Effectively use their wider knowledge of children's literature and other texts to enrich children's experience and pleasure in reading
- Let children control more of their own reading and exercise their rights as readers
- Make time and space for children to explore texts in greater depth, share favourites and talk spontaneously about their reading
- Build reciprocal and interactive communities of readers.

(The Open University Reading for Pleasure Pedagogy: https://ourfp.org/reading-for-pleasure-pedagogy/)

So while we cannot make children enjoy reading, we can create the conditions in which they are more likely to find pleasure in reading. In Chapter 2, we will explore some of the physical and organisational aspects of a positive reading environment, while in this chapter the focus will be on the role of the teacher. Children need to see that their teachers are readers who know a range of stories and poems, and are willing and able to discuss them in a positive and thoughtful way. This means finding out what children enjoy reading and gaining a wider knowledge of what might engage them. It also involves introducing children to texts and whetting their appetites to read more. One way of doing this is to use a model similar to that seen in cinemas, where the main feature is preceded by a series of adverts for other films. Short, exciting excerpts are shown with a commentary designed to make the audience want to see the whole film. In the classroom, we can choose extracts from books we think children might enjoy and 'advertise' them by reading selected passages aloud. Of course, it's important to ensure that there are copies available so that children can get access to them before their enthusiasm wanes. One colleague, who also ran the school bookshop, always made sure she had a good stock of the texts which she would share in assembly when it was her turn to lead it.

As Leland et al. maintained: 'We think of reading aloud as a type of advertising for literacy that gets listeners interested in topics, books and reading in general' (2018: 17). In the next sections, we will look at ways of developing our awareness of children's literature and of sharing it with children, in particular through reading aloud to them.

Reading aloud

The author, Neil Gaiman (2013), stated that we have an obligation to read aloud to our children.: 'To read them things they enjoy. To read them stories we are already tired of. To do the voices and not stop reading to them just because they learn to read to themselves. Use reading-aloud time as bonding time ... when the distractions of the world are put aside.'

In this section, we will look at the benefits of reading aloud and the justifications for making it an integral part of reading pedagogy. The National Curriculum states that 'pupils should continue to have opportunities to listen frequently to stories, poems, nonfiction and other writing, including whole books and not just extracts, so that they build on what was taught previously' (DfE, 2013: 38). This is reinforced in the Year 5/6 non-statutory notes and guidance, which comments:

> Even though pupils can now read independently, reading aloud to them should include whole books so that they meet books and authors that they might not choose to read themselves.
>
> (DfE, 2013: 45)

Reading aloud to children enables them to engage with texts which they might not otherwise be able to enjoy. Even weak and non-readers can follow stories which are read to them. Think about some of the plays you studied at school. Perhaps you looked at Shakespeare's plays and found the language difficult to penetrate, but maybe you then saw a production of the play at a theatre where skilled actors brought the play to life and you began to understand what it was about. Hearing text being read by a skilled reader who knows how to bring a story or poem to life through accurate and expressive reading can do the same, and can inspire children to want to read independently, even when the vocabulary and grammar of text may be challenging. As Mayer puts it, 'It is not only reading-aloud, it is staging emotions, it is creating a space of literature based on cultural interaction and learning, it is a way to encounter and create dialogic meaning' (2020: 180).

Exposing children to text which would otherwise be difficult for them to follow also offers opportunities for discussion about vocabulary, language usage and events. As Clements (2018: 16) maintains:

> Both at home and at school, listening to books being read aloud introduces children to words and language that perhaps they wouldn't be able to or choose to read independently yet. It also helps them to hear what fluent reading sounds like and to hear the pronunciation of unfamiliar words.

Research focus: The value of reading aloud to children

There is evidence which indicates that children who are read to regularly 'enter school with larger vocabularies and more advanced comprehension skills than their peers who grow up in poorer home literacy environments' (Mol and Bus, 2011: 268). The DfE's 2021 Reading Framework cites studies which put figures to the assertions. For example, Logan et al. (2019) looked at the numbers of words in early reading books and estimated that children who are never read to at home are exposed to approximately 300,000 fewer words than children who are read to once a day from birth to 5 years of age.

In a news release about the same study, *ScienceDaily* in the USA highlighted the impact of parents reading with children. It asserted that children would have heard vastly different numbers of words, depending upon how often they were read to: 'by the time they were 5 years old: Never read to, 4,662 words; 1–2 times per week, 63,570 words; 3–5 times per week, 169,520 words; daily, 296,660 words; and five books a day, 1,483,300 words' (Ohio State University, 2019).

Case study: Developing a reading aloud culture

Following an Ofsted inspection report which was critical of variations in provision of reading aloud, staff at a 250-pupil primary school organised a training day with a focus on sharing texts with children. They invited a children's author who regularly visited schools to share his books with Key Stage 2 (KS2) children, and he began the day by reading sections from his and other authors' work. He read each text in a different style, sometimes using a range of accents, sometimes varying voice level, sometimes moving around as he read, and sometimes asking questions about the text. He then asked staff to consider in groups whether they had been engaged by the reading and why, and what else he could have done to make the texts more engaging. To encourage candour, he invited them to write their comments anonymously on Post-it notes and stick them on a board during a coffee break.

After the break, the author reviewed some of the comments and found that some people enjoyed the use of different accents and various dramatic effects, while others preferred the reader to sit still and read with expression. Some staff admitted that they felt uncomfortable about varying their voices and adopting different accents for different characters. The author reassured them that it was not essential to use different voices, but that using different tones of voice often helped bring text to life. He asked staff to work with partners and to read to each other and provide feedback and suggestions for developing reading aloud. He noted that the school had adopted a 'three stars and a wish' approach to marking children's work and suggested that staff use this approach when commenting to colleagues on their reading aloud.

After lunch, there was feedback from staff, most of whom said they had actually enjoyed the experience of reading aloud and had found their colleagues' feedback positive and helpful. Discussion around one table had led teachers from different classes to offer to read to each other's classes, as well as their own. Another group said that their main concern was finding books which would engage children's interest. Some of the teachers reported that they had not enjoyed reading aloud because the stories they had tried hadn't aroused children's enthusiasm.

The author emphasised the importance of reading texts themselves before reading them to children, and encouraged them to do the following in preparation:

- Note where you might ask a question
- Find cliff-hangers where you can end the reading session leaving children eager to find out what happens next
- Look carefully at dialogue to ensure you know from the verbs and adverbs used how things were said

In the final part of the training day, the author asked staff to consider what kinds of texts they felt should be read aloud to children. Before reading the teachers' responses, think about what your choices would be.

Activity

What kinds of texts should be read aloud to children? Think of types of texts rather than specific stories, poems, etc.

Case study: What should be read aloud?

Teachers were asked to discuss texts in groups organised around the age groups they taught. Each group was asked to produce a short PowerPoint presentation which could be shared with the whole staff and could be drawn upon in subsequent staff meetings.

The choices of at least two of the four groups can be summarised as follows:

- Books which include high quality illustrations which can be shared with children. This was felt to be particularly important for children whose first language was not English, so that they had a better chance of understanding a story.
- Stories with central characters the children can relate to, including those from similar areas or backgrounds.
- Stories and poems which feature Black Asian and minority ethnic (BAME) characters. It was stressed by one group that these should include those where characters' ethnicity was not an issue, in the same way that it would usually be irrelevant in stories which featured central characters who were white.
- Stories and poems written by people from different countries and ethnicities.
- Books which extend knowledge of lifestyles, cultures and values to promote discussion and awareness.
- Stories which they might consider too difficult for children to read independently.
- Stories and poems which the reader/teacher likes. Staff commented that children tended to respond well when it was clear that their teacher was enjoying a story too.
- Books about subjects which children might not otherwise read about, including stories which help develop understanding of other subjects, such as history.

Other suggestions made by one of the groups included:

- Books which extend children's knowledge of literature, including children's classics
- Biographies of famous people
- Non-fiction
- Stories which include LGBQT+ characters

It was suggested, and agreed, that everyone would contribute example texts to a display in the staffroom in order to broaden people's awareness of available texts.

Finding recommended literature

The BookTrust (www.booktrust.org.uk) is the UK's largest reading charity dedicated to sharing books, resources and support to get every child reading, regularly and by choice. It operates in every region in England, Northern Ireland and Wales, working through every local authority, via children's centres, schools, libraries and health professionals, to reach the families who need it most.

The website provides suggestions and recommendations for different age groups, including all-time favourites and new texts. It also has a very useful section called *What to Read After*, which recommends stories which children who have enjoyed one book might enjoy next.

Activity

Find a story which you would consider reading to your class. Use a voice recorder to record yourself reading a section of the story. A few days later, listen to the recording and ask yourself the following questions:

- Did I read with expression?
- Could I tell which characters were speaking from the different tones I used?
- Was I able to listen to the story and enjoy it, without being constantly conscious of my reading?
- At what points might it be appropriate to pause to discuss events with children?
- What did I do well and what could I improve?

A development of this activity could be to make voice recordings of stories for children to listen to independently while following the text. These recordings might also be useful resources for children who have prolonged absences from school, and could be linked to activities for children and parents and carers. During a lockdown in 2020, teachers at a school in County Durham recorded bedtime stories for pupils and made them available via the school website, while also providing suggestions for discussing the stories.

What is special about stories?

Stories are at the heart of our culture. There has probably never been a culture or civilisation which has not developed a lore, a mythology or story-bank of its own, way before the development of literacy and written forms. When we meet people and tell them about things which happened to us and to others, we are telling stories. If we tell a joke, we are telling a story. Our everyday language often includes references to well-known stories and characters: think Cinderella, crying wolf, tortoise and the hare, Scrooge, and many others. Stories are part of our cultural heritage.

Once we see this, we start to realise that everything is, or has, a story. Traditionally, most of us would think a story has a beginning, a middle and an end – but think how many stories start with a flashback. And in most stories of the type in which a mystery or puzzle of some kind is gradually solved, there is a mixing of time sequences in which, while the narrative moves forward, the truths being uncovered reach back further and further as the investigation goes on. Stories can be told in different ways, too: the two most usual are either by a third-person narrator who is outside the action, or a first-person narration by one of the characters. This second style can be annoying to some readers, because of the awareness that whatever happens, the narrator will be fine and will survive to tell the story. (This convention can be played with, though; one of Agatha Christie's best-selling murder mysteries reveals on the last page that the trusty narrator was in fact the murderer all the time!)

A story featuring a character we can identify strongly with can help us confirm that our thoughts, reactions and ideas are normal and we are not alone. A story with situations and characters from outside our own experience opens our eyes to other lives, other ways of thinking and seeing the world. Both types add enormously to the enrichment of our own mental and emotional development.

The author Stephen King, in his memoir, described books as 'a uniquely portable magic' (2002: 3). Once children realise that Narnia, Dictionopolis or the Neverland, Hogwarts, Middle Earth or the Hundred Acre Wood will always be there as soon as they open the covers, the magic is working. Our job is to show them this truth.

This chapter focuses on the intrinsic pleasure of reading and for some this might preclude providing activities and questions associated with texts, which might break the 'uniquely portable magic spell'. However, if associated activities can deepen understanding of characters, settings and events, they may add to the pleasure of reading. In Chapter 3, we will explore some potential approaches in more detail, but it is worth considering a few possible questions linked to texts at this stage.

- What would you do in that situation?
- What do you think will happen next?
- Which characters do you like and why?

Another strategy to get children thinking about a story and discussing it with others is to ask them to work in pairs or threes to summarise the story so far in, say, six words. This does not have to be a sentence or a phrase and could simply comprise nouns, or nouns and verbs. For example, can you tell which story openings are described below?

Jack mother cow market magic beans
Girl grandmother woods visit basket wolf
Cinderella cruel sisters work sad invitation
Children woods breadcrumbs cottage sweets witch

You may have looked at the six-word accounts and disagreed with some of the vocabulary choices and you may wish to provide alternative versions. By asking children to share their ideas and perhaps by producing a whole-class six-word account, you can encourage discussion and justification of choices. The six-word stories can also be used as notes to help children retell stories orally, perhaps to members of other classes.

Not only is this a good way of getting children thinking about the key elements of stories, but it also a useful method of developing their ability to make notes. Children's discussions of the story books which they read can enable them to gain a greater insight into the ways in which texts are constructed and may allow them to develop their abilities to read critically and to write more adventurously. Further suggestions are made below.

Exploring fiction with children

Monk, Davies and Karavis suggested that analysing a novel with children can afford them various levels of understanding, for example:

> 1. Reading what is in the text, retelling what has been read.
> 2. Reading between the lines, considering possible or implied meanings.
> 3. Making associations with other knowledge, experience and reading.
> 4. Reflecting on what has been read, re-evaluating responses and perhaps modifying beliefs and understanding.
>
> (Monk et al., 1994: 32)

This approach demands that children gain a deeper level of understanding of what they read than might be acquired simply through independent reading, and it requires teacher involvement and knowledge of the stories which the pupils read.

One approach could involve a series of activities related to a text which are introduced gradually, perhaps as a story is being read to the children in serial form. Initially, children could be asked to speculate about what the story might be about, basing their predictions upon features of the book such as the cover, the publisher's blurb, the contents page and the first page. They could also take into account any knowledge which they might have of other works by the same author.

As the story progresses, children might be invited to make further predictions and could be asked for their views on the ways in which different characters behave. Character grids or charts might be produced with illustrations. Children could be asked to provide adjectives which describe each of the main characters and to write about the person whom they like most, or the one whom they would most like to be if they were part of the story.

Before the story is completed, the children might, on more than one occasion, be asked to write their own chapter endings or the ending for the story which they would like or which they predict. As they discover the author's version, they could compare it with their own versions and consider which they find most satisfactory.

Further activities could include making relationship charts (see Hunt, 1995: 35–36), which show how characters are related to each other by family ties or by actions. It may be useful at this point to discuss some of the soap operas the children watch and to ask them how they think the authors keep track of the characters' histories. They might also select a few of the principal soap characters and produce charts which show on which occasions they had dealings with each other. Relating the activity to television programmes may appear to deviate from literacy development, but it may well engender interest in some children who might otherwise have been reluctant participants. By moving from the familiar to the less familiar, children may gain a greater insight into methods of analysing stories.

The plot of the story book may be analysed and discussed in various ways. Children might produce a list of key events or a timeline to show the sequence of events. They could draw a story board and make notes on what is depicted in their pictures. They could the use their story boards as a starting point for dramatising the story. They might be encouraged to select key passages from the story and compare their ideas on what the major events were. They could also select particularly exciting passages and use these to advertise the book in the same way that film-makers take exciting parts of films and use them in promotional extracts on videos and at the cinema.

A further activity might involve the children in selecting passages of speech and copying out and displaying these so that others could examine them and try to decide who the speakers were. They could go on to write further dialogue in the style in which different characters might have spoken when discussing events which the author describes, but for which he or she does not write dialogue.

Once the book has been read, pupils could be asked to consider what could happen to the characters in the future. For example, they could be asked to write about a further adventure for one person.

Another activity would be to retell the story in a concise way, perhaps in a mini-saga or drabble (a short work of fiction of precisely one hundred words in length) with a strict word limit (see Waugh and McGuinn, 1996: 35–36 and 118). Here children would be encouraged to think carefully about the key events and use words economically to tell the story. They might go on to discuss the merits of writing at greater length in order to make the story more interesting for the reader.

Having examined the publisher's blurb on the back of the book before reading the story, the children could return to it afterwards and rewrite it in their own way. They could design an alternative book cover (see Waugh and McGuinn, 1996: 52) and consider ways of making the book attractive and enticing to potential readers. Children may also be invited to produce alternative endings for the story and compare these with the original. Discussions could centre around children's interpretations of the fates which they felt each character deserved.

Analysis of texts may appear potentially dull, and some may argue that such an activity could detract from pupils' enjoyment of the story. However, their pleasure may be enhanced if the activities are made interesting and exciting and if they afford children opportunities to gain a greater insight into their reading. This can be initiated by teachers and other adults, but may also involve children in leading book-talk. In the case study below, we see how teachers developed reading partnerships between pupils of different ages, which fostered sharing of texts and discussion about them.

Case study: Reading partners

When Saffi took up her post as Literacy Coordinator at a one-form entry rural primary school, she audited the children's reading habits and was concerned that quite a few of them rarely read for pleasure. SATs scores over recent years had generally been good and it was clear from working with her Year 6 class that most children were competent, if not particularly enthusiastic, readers.

Saffi wanted to promote a culture of reading for pleasure and develop both staff and pupils' enthusiasm for this. She discussed her ideas with a colleague, Kyle, who taught in Year 2 and who shared Saffi's concerns and complained that once children reached KS2, there seemed to be an emphasis on teaching the mechanics of reading at the expense of developing positive attitudes to reading. Kyle and Saffi decided to develop a reading partnership programme which would involve Year 6 children being paired with Year 2 children once a week to share books. They decided that this would involve:

- Children reading to each other
- Children sharing and discussing favourite books
- Encouraging children to prepare by creating questions
- Children visiting the school library in their pairs to look for new books

The emphasis was to be on enjoyment. The Year 6 children's role was to share and talk about books; it was not to teach reading, even though the Year 2 children might acquire some additional reading skills by being exposed to texts they would not be able to read by themselves.

The weekly sessions were popular with both Year 2 and Year 6 and an interesting outcome was a growth in confidence among some of the older children who either lacked confidence or enthusiasm for reading. Many Year 6 children also enjoyed revisiting books they had read in KS1.

By developing children's engagement with texts and giving them opportunities to discuss them, Saffi and her colleague found that both the Year 2 and Year 6 children enjoyed reading more. She was also able to show her colleagues that such partnerships could enable meeting National Curriculum requirements.

Link to National Curriculum

Pupils should be taught to:

- participate in discussion about books, poems and other works that are read to them and those that they can read for themselves, taking turns and listening to what others say
- explain and discuss their understanding of books, poems and other material, both those that they listen to and those that they read for themselves

(Year 2 Programme of Study, DfE, 2013: 28)

- participate in discussions about books that are read to them and those they can read for themselves, building on their own and others' ideas and challenging views courteously

(Years 5 and 6 Programme of Study, DfE, 2013: 44)

Incentives to read

Finally, the focus of this chapter has been on the intrinsic pleasures of reading: on reading as an activity we do because we enjoy it and want to do it. Some children seldom or never experience reading for pleasure, but schools recognise that they need to build their reading stamina if they are to develop their literacy skills. This can lead to them devising a range of incentives or extrinsic motivations for reading. We have seen schools which have competitions with points awarded to children being 'caught' reading in unusual places (hanging upside down from the climbing frame was one example), and one with a 'walk of fame' on the concrete path from the school gate to its entrance. Children who had read 100 books had their names painted within stars on the paving stones, Hollywood-style. While this may elevate the status of reading for some and perhaps draw attention to a range of texts, it is important that children regard reading as having intrinsic rather than simply extrinsic reward. Alexander and Jarman (2018: 85) summarised the pleasures derived from reading science non-fiction as ranging from extrinsic to intrinsic:

- extrinsic comprised rewards such as stickers and certificates;
- both extrinsic and intrinsic included book-talk, social reading – book-based activities;
- intrinsic was simply delight in the book in itself.

Cremin, however, sounds a cautious note about extrinsic incentives, which provides a fitting final comment for a chapter which has focused on the intrinsic pleasures of reading:

> In-class or school competitions with awards for the number of books read, reviews written and parent signatures in reading records, for instance, have recently become popular. The resultant prizes (a Friday film and popcorn, for example, for the class with the highest percentage of parents' signatures) are positioned as incentives, but such extrinsic motivators rarely work in the long term. They encourage children to read for recognition, for reward, for their parents, their teachers and/or the school, but not for themselves. Reading for pleasure is more closely associated with intrinsic motivation; it is reading that children do for themselves at their own pace, with whom they choose and in their own way.
>
> (Cremin, 2019: 5)

In Chapter 2, we will explore ways of creating an environment in which reading for pleasure can flourish.

Learning outcomes review

By reading this chapter, you have considered:

- The importance of making reading a pleasurable activity for children
- How teachers can introduce children to texts which they might not be able to read independently
- The value of stories and some simple ways of engaging children's interest in them

Questions for discussion

- Do most children in your school read for pleasure?
- Are you aware of the tastes and preferences of your children as readers?
- Do you have sufficient knowledge of children's literature to be able to guide children towards texts they might enjoy?
- How confident do you feel about reading aloud to a class?

For your bookshelf

Rowling, J.K. (2003) *Harry Potter and the Order of the Phoenix*. London: Bloomsbury. The fifth book of the Harry Potter series, it follows the hero's fifth year at Hogwarts School of Witchcraft and Wizardry. Harry and his cousin Dudley are attacked by Dementors and Harry is expelled from Hogwarts after using magic to fend them off, but his expulsion is postponed pending a hearing at the Ministry of Magic. Like the rest of the series, there is a popular film of the book which adheres closely to Rowling's original story.

Further reading

Gill, A., Stephenson, M. and Waugh, D. (eds.) (2021) *Developing a Love of Reading and Books.* London: Learning Matters.

Waugh, D. (2015) How Danny, the Champion of the World saved my career, *Teach Primary*, issue #85. Available at https://www.teachprimary.com/learning_resources/view/how-danny-the-champion-of-the-world-saved-my-career (accessed 21 February 2022).

Waugh, D., Neaum, S. and Waugh, R. (2016) *Children's Literature in Primary Schools.* London: Sage.

References

Alexander, J. and Jarman, R. (2018) The pleasures of reading non-fiction, *Literacy*, 52 (2): 78–85.

All-Party Parliamentary Group for Education (APPG) (2011) *Report of the Inquiry into Overcoming the Barriers to Literacy.* Available at: http://www.educationengland.org.uk/documents/pdfs/2011-appge-literacy-report.pdf (accessed 13 July 2021).

BBC News (2020) Marcus Rashford launches children's book club to spread joy of reading, *BBC News*, 17 November. Available at: https://www.bbc.co.uk/news/entertainment-arts-54972339 (accessed 13 July 2021).

Clark, C. and Teravainen-Goff, A. (2020) *Children and Young People's Reading in 2019: Findings from our annual literacy study.* London: National Literacy Trust. Available at: https://literacytrust.org.uk/research-services/research-reports/children-and-young-peoples-reading-in-2019/ (accessed 25 August 2021).

Clements, J. (2018) Reading and language acquisition, in *Why Closing the Word Gap Matters: Oxford Language Report.* Oxford: Oxford University Press. Available at: https://www.oup.com.cn/test/word-gap.pdf (accessed 23 September 2021).

Cremin, T. (2019) Reading communities: Why, what and how?, *NATE Primary Matters Magazine*, Summer. Available at: https://oro.open.ac.uk/60382/1/P4-8_Reading%20Communities%20Teresa%20Cremin_Final.pdf.

Cremin, T. (2021) Building communities of engaged readers, in A. Gill, M. Stephenson and D. Waugh (eds.) *Developing a Love of Reading and Books.* London: Learning Matters.

Department for Education (DfE) (2011) *Teachers' Standards: Guidance for school leaders, school staff and governing bodies* (updated 2013 and 2021). London: DfE. Available at: https://www.gov.uk/government/publications/teachers-standards.

Department for Education (DfE) (2013) *The National Curriculum in England: Key Stages 1 and 2 framework document.* London: DfE. Available at: https://www.gov.uk/government/publications/national-curriculum-in-england-primary-curriculum (accessed 30 July 2021).

Department for Education (DfE) (2021) *The Reading Framework: Teaching the foundations of literacy.* London: DfE. Available at: https://assets.publishing.service.gov.uk/government/uploads/system/uploads/attachment_data/file/1000986/Reading_framework_Teaching_the_foundations_of_literacy_-_July-2021.pdf (accessed 15 August 2021).

Gaiman, N. (2013) Why our future depends on libraries, reading and daydreaming, *The Guardian*, 15 October. Available at: https://www.theguardian.com/books/2013/oct/15/neil-gaiman-future-libraries-reading-daydreaming?CMP=share_btn_tw (accessed 25 August 2021).

Hunt, G. (1995) *Reading KS2 (Curriculum Bank)*. Leamington Spa: Scholastic.

King, S. (2002) *On Writing: A Memoir of the Craft*. New York: Pocket Books.

Leland, C.H. and Lewison, M. with Harste, J.C. (2018) *Teaching Children's Literature: It's Critical*, 2nd edition. Abingdon: Routledge.

Logan, J.A.R., Justice, L.M., Yumuş, M. and Chaparro-Moreno, L.J. (2019) When children are not read to at home: The Million Word Gap, *Journal of Developmental and Behavioral Pediatrics*, 40 (5): 373–386.

Mangan, L. (2018) *Bookworm: A Memoir of Childhood Reading*. London: Square Peg.

Mayer, J. (2020) Reading books as shared events: A performative view on early literacy practices, *Filoteknos*, 10: 162–184. Available at: http://www.ifp2.uni.wroc.pl/wp-content/uploads/Filoteknos/Filoteknos10/filotek.10-12.pdf (accessed 15 February 2022).

McGrane, J., Stiff, J., Baird, J.-A., Lenkeit, J. and Hopfenbeck, T. (2017) *Progress in International Reading Literacy Study (PIRLS): National report for England*. London: Department of Education. Available at: https://assets.publishing.service.gov.uk/government/uploads/system/uploads/attachment_data/file/664562/PIRLS_2016_National_Report_for_England-_BRANDED.pdf (accessed 15 February 2022).

Mol, S.E. and Bus, A.G. (2011) To read or not to read: A meta-analysis of print exposure from infancy to early adulthood, *Psychological Bulletin*, 137 (2): 267–296.

Monk, J., Davies, P. and Karavis, S. (1994) Becoming a Reader: 3, *Language and Learning*, January/February: 32–35.

Ohio State University (2019) A 'million word gap' for children who aren't read to at home: That's how many fewer words some may hear by kindergarten, *ScienceDaily*, 4 April. Available at: www.sciencedaily.com/releases/2019/04/190404074947.htm (accessed 23 September 2021).

Rashford, Marcus (2020) BBC News https://www.bbc.co.uk/news/entertainment-arts-54972339. 17.11.20)

Waugh, D. with McGuinn, N. (1996) *Curriculum Bank Writing at Key Stage 2*. Leamington Spa: Scholastic.

2 Creating an environment in which children's literature is valued

"Social reading environments were seen to be key to creating richly reciprocal reading communities in the Teachers as Readers research. Physically engaging, the most successful environments tempted children into texts and offered spaces to relax, browse, and read for pleasure."

– Open University Reading for Pleasure website

Learning outcomes

After reading this chapter, you will have considered:

- The physical environment of the classroom and the school and how it can be developed to ensure children's literature is valued
- Strategies to promote reading for pleasure and the development of reading skills
- Ways in which children can take ownership of areas of the classroom and school to ensure that reading is valued
- How other adults can support children's reading development and engagement with children's literature

Link to the Teachers' Standards

1. Set high expectations which inspire, motivate and challenge pupils

- establish a safe and stimulating environment for pupils, rooted in mutual respect

5. Adapt teaching to respond to the strengths and needs of all pupils

- have a secure understanding of how a range of factors can inhibit pupils' ability to learn, and how best to overcome these

- have a clear understanding of the needs of all pupils, including those with special educational needs; those of high ability; those with English as an additional language; those with disabilities; and be able to use and evaluate distinctive teaching approaches to engage and support them

8. Fulfil wider professional responsibilities

- communicate effectively with parents with regard to pupils' achievements and well-being

(DfE, 2011: 10–13)

Link to the National Curriculum

Schools should do everything to promote wider reading. They should provide library facilities and set ambitious expectations for reading at home.

(DfE, 2013: 10)

The overarching aim for English in the national curriculum is to promote high standards of language and literacy by equipping pupils with a strong command of the spoken and written word, and to develop their love of literature through widespread reading for enjoyment.

(DfE, 2013: 13)

In Chapter 1, we explored facets of developing children's intrinsic pleasure in reading and discussed the importance of introducing them to a range of stimulating texts. We stressed the importance of reading to them and engaging their interest. But it is not enough simply to read to children and talk with them about literature, we also need to create a literate environment so that children's literature is an integral part of the classroom and the wider school. This chapter will include examples of things you can do to create a classroom which is physically literate, and will explore strategies for listening to readers, developing comprehension, and involving parents, carers and families in children's reading development. We will also explore the potential of school libraries, and will look at ways to engage children's families in their literacy development. We will begin with the concept of a literate classroom and describe the steps a newly qualified teacher took in her first permanent appointment.

Case study: Creating a literate classroom

Sara was a recently qualified teacher who had taken a one-term contract, gained more permanent employment for the spring term and joined a small primary school with four classes. She wanted to create a classroom for her Year 4/5s in which children's literature and texts more generally could be prized and celebrated. The room she inherited had been in general use and had few displays, and had only become a classroom due to expanding pupil numbers. Sara's class of 16 had been created by putting the eight oldest Year 4s from an existing Year 3/4 class and the eight youngest Year 5s from an existing Year 5/6 class, so she was conscious that two groups of children would be coming together to form her class. She was also aware that some of the parents of the Year 5 children were unhappy at the perception that their children had been 'moved down' a class and given an inexperienced teacher. Sara was, therefore, eager to make the classroom as welcoming and attractive as possible in order to create an inviting environment for the children. However, she decided, after consulting an experienced teacher who was a member of her family, that it was also important to leave scope for the children to work together as a team to put their own mark on the classroom.

Sara therefore decided that she would put up some displays for general reference, such as charts of synonyms for *nice* and alternatives to using *said* in dialogue. She also copied and displayed covers of some of her favourite children's books together with copies of the opening pages. Finally, she created a small area with a desk, chair, lamp, bookshelf and display board, which she labelled *Miss Bentley's Reading Corner*. She put copies of the books on the shelf and put a selection of texts she had read in the last week on the display board. These included newspapers, timetables, league tables, TV listings, crosswords and codewords, and leaflets and brochures she picked up from the local Tourist Information office. She then set aside four other areas in the classroom for children to create their own reading areas in teams.

When the children arrived, Sara drew attention to her reading area and told them she wanted them to work in teams of four, each comprising two Year 4s and two Year 5s, to design their own reading corners. The headteacher had made some money available to buy bean bags, shelves, books and so forth, and she provided them with a budget of £100 per group and access to an online catalogue. Groups were given opportunities to share ideas with each other and with the whole class, and after two weeks plans had been finalised and purchases made. Three groups bought bean bags and all purchased a small selection of books. Shelf units were made by two parents and each group chose a reading lamp. The school provided a laptop for each reading corner. Display boards included two 'reading rivers' and two charts on which children displayed copies of things they had read recently. These included:

- Adverts
- Book covers
- Recommendations
- Excerpts from texts to match to book covers
- Pictures of authors and biographies
- Sports reports
- TV listings

- Weather forecasts
- Book quizzes
- Newspaper articles about local and national events

Sara felt that getting the class involved in working together to design their reading areas had helped the children to bond and become a class unit. They took pride in their reading areas and invited people from other groups to spend time in them. As well as setting aside time in the school day for children to use the areas, Sara encouraged children to use them when they had completed work. The areas were constantly added to and displays and texts were changed regularly. Sara was delighted with the positive feedback from parents and carers at a parents' evening at the end of the Spring term. Indeed, one parent, who was also a primary teacher and literacy coordinator, said that she would like to introduce some of Sara's ideas into her own classroom and asked Sara's permission to take photographs of the classroom so that she could share these with colleagues.

The parent and Sara agreed to meet to discuss potential cooperation between their schools and each approached their headteachers to discuss a possible CPD event focused on creating a literate environment. Although this was delayed due to Covid-19 lockdowns and school closures, a workshop eventually took place and all teachers were asked to share an example of something they had done to help create a literate environment. Examples of these are presented below.

Anatomy of a book

One teacher explained how she made use of books which were damaged and would otherwise have been removed from the class library by taking them to pieces to create displays of the anatomy of a book. The displays were labelled and features displayed included: book cover, back cover and blurb, biographical notes on the author, title page, contents, book details page with publisher, place and date of publication, etc., story opening, example of dialogue, and a couple of exciting sections from the opening chapter. The teacher explained that she always made sure that she bought or borrowed intact copies of the books she used in this way, so that children's appetite for reading them could be satisfied.

'Adult' texts

Another teacher found that children enjoyed looking at texts which were not necessarily written for children, but which focused on things which interested them. He had displayed natural science books by David Attenborough and travel books by Michael Palin, and found that many children were captivated by the photographs and some went on to read sections of the books.

Books I got for Christmas

A Year 1/2 teacher created an annual display in January of books children had received at Christmas time. She asked children to bring in copies to talk with others about, and made a display of book covers by copying images from online booksellers. Children were not asked to write a review of their books, but were invited to write their own blurb to try to persuade others to read them.

Stories told using PowerPoint

During a lockdown when most children were at home, two Reception/KS1 teachers created presentations featuring pictures from story books and recorded voiceovers to accompany slides. These were made available via the school's website, together with topics for discussion which parents might use with their children. The presentations were popular and continued to be used once children were back in school.

Book packs

A Year 5/6 teacher, Moheen, shared examples of box files he had created containing pictures and artefacts associated with different children's novels. He had based his idea on the book sacks containing artefacts relevant to stories, which early years colleagues used when reading to children. However, he felt these might not appeal to older children and decided to create materials which might appeal to more mature readers and could engage their interest in the background to stories. He also wanted the packs to be small enough to be portable, so that children could take them home to examine with family members. Moheen shared an example for Michael Morpurgo's *Private Peaceful*, which included laminated photographs of First World War soldiers, trenches, medals and maps.

Sharing a story via Zoom

Two Year 3 and Year 4 teachers had read stories to children via Zoom during lockdowns. Although they found that some children seemed easily distracted, they reported that most welcomed the stories and the social contact with a teacher and fellow pupils. One teacher had found an article which described a successful virtual classroom created by a student teacher, and provided a link for colleagues.

Activity

Make a note of some of the good practice you have seen in creating an environment in which children's literature is valued. Discuss what you have seen with colleagues and note any ideas which you would like to put into practice in your own classroom.

Research focus: A virtual classroom

Paige Brown, a trainee teacher at the University of Worcester, created a virtual classroom for teaching on Zoom during her school placement. She describes in articles she wrote for educational magazines how she developed attractive backgrounds and asserts:

> Sharing your virtual scene whilst teaching on Zoom can bring a sense of warmth to the online environment, instead of the children staring into the empty black squares. I have found that it makes the children feel relaxed when they join the lesson but still promotes good learning behaviour by keeping them on task.
>
> (Brown, 2021: 31)

Just like a real classroom, the virtual classroom can be adapted for different activities. As Paige maintained:

> Your virtual classroom is of course editable so keep that creativity flowing. I like to change my main virtual space every week, either adding in an additional detail, moving furniture or even bringing in a pet!
>
> (Brown, 2021: 31)

Paige's initiative was followed by colleagues who urged her to share her experiences more widely. There is clear potential here for creating a literate environment for teaching and learning, even when children cannot be in school. And while it is hoped that lockdowns will not become a regular occurrence which will necessitate teaching in virtual classrooms, there is potential here for supporting children who are absent through illness or other reasons.

Just as we might modify a virtual classroom to keep it fresh and interesting, it is important to make actual classrooms and reading areas flexible and fluid and to involve children in creating appealing venues for working.

Time to read

Most primary schools set aside time for quiet or silent reading: a period when everyone, including teachers and support staff in many cases, reads quietly and independently. Many schools give these sessions catchy names and acronyms, and these include:

DEAR: Drop Everything And Read
SQUIRT: Sustained Quiet Uninterrupted Reading Time
ERIC: Everyone Reading in Class

In many classrooms these sessions are quiet, peaceful occasions which provide an opportunity for everyone to become absorbed in reading. In others, some children seem to spend most of the period changing books or finding other ways of avoiding actually reading. Our observations suggest that quiet reading sessions are more focused when teachers and support staff join in and read themselves, while those which are more disrupted are often the ones in which adults spend the time listening to readers or performing other tasks which break the silence. While finding time in a busy day to support individual readers is challenging and quiet reading time provides a rare opportunity to do this, it should be remembered that children reading aloud to adults in an otherwise silent or near silent room will be displaying all of their reading errors for their classmates to hear. This may have a damaging effect upon their self-esteem as developing readers. It may, therefore, be worth considering listening to readers outside the classroom during quiet reading times.

Quiet reading times can be made more appealing when children are able to read in different places away from their desks or tables. Having a carpeted area with bean bags or comfortable chairs not only allows children to read in comfort, but also gives the teacher the chance of offering a treat as an incentive for children to focus on their reading and be rewarded for doing so. Similarly, the creation of a reading area or the use of a school library can make quiet reading seem special and more appealing.

The 2021 Reading Framework maintains that the selection of books available in reading areas is more important than the way the area is decorated and states:

> Ideally, every book corner should be a mini-library, a place for children to browse the best books, revisit the ones that the teacher has read to them, and borrow books to read or retell at home. Every child should be able to spend time in their book corner. Children will want to share books with others, especially if they are 'books in common' that they know their friends have heard before.
>
> (DfE, 2021: 33)

As well as guiding them to high quality reading material in the classroom, some teachers allow children to choose their own reading material for quiet reading, either on every occasion or on one day a week. This might mean that children bring in annuals, comics, digital texts or newspapers, and it emphasises reading as a purposeful and pleasurable activity.

The value of libraries

Alec Williams' *Get Everyone Reading* (2021) points out that one in eight schools don't have a library and stresses their value. He quotes author Nicola Morgan, who stated: 'Libraries are greenhouses for brains.' In this section, we look at the value of school libraries and at one school's approach to improving its library.

Research focus: Libraries

Teravainen and Clark (2017) conducted a literature review to produce a comprehensive contemporary picture of school libraries in the UK and their impact on pupils' learning. Among their key findings were that school libraries were found to:

- impact pupils' general academic attainment, reading and writing skills, plus wider learning skills, as well as their scores in history, mathematics and science.
- have an impact on pupils' reading enjoyment, reading behaviour and attitudes towards reading. Motivation and attitudes in particular have been connected to school library use.

Interestingly, the benefits of school libraries extended to:

- personal and interpersonal outcomes, such as self-esteem and the feeling of success and accomplishment, have also been associated with school library use.

(Teravainen and Clark, 2017: 3)

In Australia, Mat Roni and Merga found that:

> increasing students' opportunities to access a library can have a strong positive influence on their reading engagement … [and that] … Interventions that enhance student access to their school libraries could be the most efficacious for enhancing student reading engagement.
>
> (Mat Roni and Merga, 2019: 17)

The research findings are backed up by Ofsted's conclusions: 'In many of the good primary schools, all classes had a weekly timetabled visit to the library. Where this happened, it had a direct impact on pupils' attitudes to reading and literacy' (2006: 19).

In the case study below, you can see how staff and pupils in one school reinvigorated its school library.

Case study: Let's Love the Library Project

Holbeach Primary School in Catford, South East London is a large school serving an ethnically and socio-economically diverse community. Assistant headteacher, Karen Robertson, leads English and the Curriculum across the school. One of the English objectives in the School Development Plan for 2019/20 was to continue to raise achievement in reading, and staff believed strongly that this was more likely if children were excited and enthused by books and reading for pleasure. Karen drew upon the Open University Teachers as Readers findings to inform discussions about ways forward.

Despite being a well-organised and attractive space, the school library had become underused. It was decided that children needed to be given greater ownership of the library and initial aims were to:

- ensure that all children had access to the library;
- find a way in which children's voices could be heard and harnessed and empower them to make changes to the organisation and resources in the library;
- give children choices and opportunities to engage in reading for pleasure in a shared, whole school environment that they had helped to create.

Expectations for using the library (all classes visit at least once per fortnight) were clarified in several staff meetings. Buddy classes were formed across the school (e.g. Year 2 and Year 6) for blogging and reading together. Gradually, the library became well used once more and there was a real buzz of excitement again.

A suggestion box was introduced and 170 notes from children were received in the first week. By the end of the first month, there had been 479 suggestions. Some of the ideas could be implemented immediately. Other requests were from children asking for specific books and authors. However, budget constraints meant that the school had to think creatively about how to provide this new reading material.

A 'Book Bus' visited the school to enable children and parents to buy books and the school bought many that the children had requested. The children decided how to categorise and display the new books in the library and the following day, the shelves were half empty. In Karen's words, 'It was as if a plague of locusts had consumed the new books!'

The library is now used regularly by classes and groups of children. Children are keen to communicate ideas for developing their library – giving them ownership has really made a difference. The library environment has been enhanced and children are eager to use it. Historically, the library was non-fiction based, where older children carried out research. Story books had been available in the classroom book corners. However, 90 per cent of the suggestions from the children requesting books were for fiction, indicating that to encourage reading for pleasure, the library needed to change. The children led that change.

So far, the project has been a great success. Children now have ownership of their school library and the way it is organised and resourced. Observations indicate that children are eager to browse, explore and discuss the books on offer, and read both independently and with others. Working closely with the children, staff have created a safe, relaxed and stimulating space where reading for pleasure is valued. This project has clearly demonstrated that, in order to make successful changes in schools, pupil voice, teamwork and creative thinking are vital.

The library will continue to evolve in response to children's ideas and feedback. Next steps will include exploring other OU Teachers as Readers findings and implementing some of the children's other suggestions, including:

- continuing to develop and extend the new fiction section with the children;
- developing new areas within the library, e.g. a book-making station where children see themselves as authors and can display their books for others to read;
- using a Recommendation Wall to ensure that children are able to share responses and opinions of books they have read;
- ensuring that independent reading time in the library continues to be comfortable, relaxing, enticing and empowering.

It is clear that Holbeach School draws upon research to inform its approach to library provision. You can find out more about findings on school libraries at the OU Teachers as Readers website and at the School Library Association website.

The school continues to explore new ways to excite and enthuse children about reading and has gone on to look at ways of extending its reading environment to the playground.

Case study: The Playground Book Club – extending reading for pleasure into the outdoor environment

Following the Let's Love the Library Project at Holbeach Primary School, in September the suggestion box was repainted gold and relaunched in assembly to maintain the interest. A huge variety of 'golden ideas' continued to be posted in 'The Box' by children. A common thread ran through many of their suggestions – requests to be able to access books at playtimes.

The Friends of Holbeach (the school's Parent Teacher Association) had worked really hard to enhance the playground, making it a greener space, full of new trees and carefully chosen plants, wooden seating and a sensory area bursting with herbs and flowers. It became clear that the school now needed to take the library outside, to develop reading areas and promote reading for pleasure in the playground.

The school partnered with a local estate agency who were able to donate over 3,000 books to source the Playground Book Club.

Two-wheeled trolleys were purchased, one for KS1 and the other for KS2 (and adapted by the premises officer to make them sturdier for use outside). Huge outdoor bean bags and snuggly blankets were also provided for comfort and warmth.

Staff from the estate agency were onsite to celebrate with staff during an exciting day of storytelling and reading workshops in the playground during the launch of the new outdoor reading club.

The children were enthused by the Playground Book Club launch and each playtime this became a very popular place to be. The children not only initiated the idea but took control of the organisation and running of it too. Several Year 6 boys offered to take responsibility for the Book Club each day; they even implemented a lending library at playtime, recording the names of children and the books being borrowed so that they could continue reading them at home!

Involving other adults

When encouraging parents, grandparents, carers and other interested and appropriate adults to come into school to support children's reading, schools often set up groups to provide guidance on how they can help. At one level this might focus on the mechanics of reading and listening to and supporting children. For example, one school provided a booklet and discussed this with volunteers before they began to work with children.

- Try to sit next to the child and hold the book together.
- Begin by talking with the child. You might talk about something unrelated to reading, or you might discuss the book the child is about to read.
- Listen to the child read a set number of pages.
- Listen to the child for a set period of time.
- Try asking the child to read a passage he or she has chosen.
- Listen to a small group of children using copies of the same book.
- Read with the child, taking turns at the instigation of the child: this is often called 'paired' reading.
- Give approving signals to the child to show that you think he or she is doing well.
- Show that you are enjoying the story: perhaps you could ask the child to read an extra page because you are interested to know what happens next.
- Finish the session with some positive remarks.
- Make a note of any difficulties the child experienced so that you or the teacher can focus on these next time.

Many schools encourage their volunteers to take part in a national programme organised by the charity Coram Beanstalk and the Open University. The sessions are free and are led by volunteer educators, including the authors of this book, Rosemary and David Waugh.

OU/Coram Beanstalk Volunteer Reading Group sessions

The focus of the workshops is broadening participants' knowledge of children's literature, and developing knowledge of how to support reading for pleasure.

These groups, which were a development of the Teachers as Readers project, which continues to hold workshops for professionals, were designed to be held in different locations around the country to support local volunteers. However, the pandemic meant that face-to-face workshops had to be abandoned and replaced by online Zoom or Teams meetings, which were open to volunteers from all over England. The programme for 2020/21 gives an indication of the content and the emphasis on reading for pleasure:

- Session 1: Choice and agency – Your knowledge of children's literature
- Session 2: The secret lives of our readers – The value of using picture books
- Session 3: Engaging reluctant readers – The joy of reading poetry
- Session 4: A community of readers – The beauty of non-fiction texts

Schools wishing to get involved can contact Coram Beanstalk at: support@corambeanstalk.org.uk

Reading at home

The focus of this book is integrating children's literature in the classroom. However, teachers and volunteers in schools are not the only people who can influence children's attitudes to reading: parents, other family members and carers play an important role too. In 2003, Desforges conducted a meta-analysis of research on parental involvement and pupil achievement. His analysis of a wide range of studies led him to conclude that, 'What parents do with their children at home through the age range, is much more significant than any other factor open to educational influence' (Desforges with Abouchaar, 2003: 91).

We should be mindful that some families are less able to support their children's reading than others, perhaps because of their own reading problems or language barriers. Where restrictions are known, schools can take steps to compensate children by giving their reading additional attention in school, but most families are able to help children with reading outside school, so it is important to provide some simple guidance on how this might be done successfully. In the case study below, you can see how a school developed a short pamphlet for home reading and provided workshops for family members.

Case study: A simple guide to reading at home

Reading at home is not just listening to your child reading a few words or pages from a reading book: reading is a part of everyday life and we can share our reading experiences with our children, from going to the shop and asking them to find items from a shopping list to looking at the TV listings, league tables, pop music charts, recipes, and so on.

Put the emphasis on reading for pleasure. Children who enjoy reading and being read to are more likely to develop their reading skills. Remember:

- It's not just what you read but where you read that affects children's engagement with reading. Try to find a quiet place away from other distractions. Make reading time special by making it comfortable and focused. Try to set aside time when the television is not on and when you will not be interrupted. Children do not enjoy reading if their favourite TV programmes are being missed!
- Texts don't always have to be challenging. As adults, we often choose to read things that are well within out reading capabilities because we enjoy them or need to find things out. Every reading session should not be a challenge designed to stretch children's reading. Let them enjoy texts which they can read easily, as well as those which stretch them. If your child occasionally brings home a book which you feel is too easy for him, do not worry.
- Read to children, as well as listening to them reading. Read along with them and help keep stories flowing by sometimes reading the words which they get stuck on rather than making them stop and sound them out. You can always revisit the words later to do this.
- Make the reading session a pleasant occasion and avoid negative comments. It is particularly hurtful for children to have their reading abilities compared unfavourably with those of brothers and sisters.
- There are lots of things you can do to make reading purposeful and enjoyable. Treasure hunts can be created indoors or outdoors with clues taking children from place to place until they find the 'treasure', which might be something they enjoy eating, a sticker, or even a toy.
- Scavenger hunts can be at different levels from single words or phrases to sentences. Children can be asked to find things around the house or garden or local park, such as a black sock, a red flower, a blue book. Once they feel confident about writing, they can make treasure and scavenger hunts for you.
- Reading in the environment is important. Take time to look at signs, labels and notices with children. Get them to help you find things at the supermarket, perhaps giving them a list of items to look for.
- Try using the subtitles facility on your television sometimes when children are watching their favourite programmes. They don't have to read all of them, but it does provide a way of showing text.
- Let us know about stories, poems and other texts which you and your child enjoyed. We welcome suggestions for additions to our libraries, including those available online.
- If you find that you really enjoy reading aloud to your children, why not come into school to read or tell stories to groups of children. If you are fortunate enough to be able to speak and read in a language besides English, you might even come and read or tell a story in that language and use visual aids to help children to follow it. If you are not able to come into school, you might consider making a recording of a story or poem to share with others.

One of the strengths of the school's guidance is an emphasis on the contribution parents can make and the encouragement to enter into dialogue about reading and contribute to reading in school. The value of engaging in a dialogue with parents so that both they and the school can support children's language development has been highlighted during Covid-19 lockdowns, as the National Literacy Trust's research confirmed.

Research focus: The impact of Covid-19 on families, and the implications for the home learning environment

In 2021, the National Literacy Trust conducted a literature review to consider the impact of Covid-19 on families, and the implications for the home learning environment. It found that some children had gained vocabulary at a faster than expected rate during lockdowns and many parents and children had enjoyed high quality experiences (Crew, 2021). However, there was considerable disparity between experiences, with children from more economically deprived backgrounds often having much less positive experiences due to lack of availability of laptops, internet access, space and parental time.

A key finding was that, 'Parents like to be listened to, have their views taken seriously, and treated as active participants in supporting their children' (Crew, 2021: 2). The report concludes that 'successful initiatives are those that focus on developing a warm and positive relationship with the family' (2021: 17).

Engaging children's interest and developing comprehension

In this chapter, we have emphasised the importance of children working together with each other and with adults. Many schools make use of cooperative learning techniques such as talk partners to encourage discussion and find that this raises the quality of responses to questions. This can be a successful strategy when talking about a class novel or poem. The Reading Framework supports such approaches:

> Pairing children with their partners, ready for responding together, encourages them to discuss a question, problem or idea and agree on their joint response. Because their answer belongs to both of them and they will have practised it first, they grow in confidence when asked to respond in front of others. The teacher can observe the pairs talking and select those with helpful answers to develop the discussion.
>
> (DfE, 2021: 24)

Cooperative approaches can be developed at more sophisticated levels, sometimes involving adults, but often only children. For more details on cooperative learning, its benefits and practical ways of working, see Jolliffe (2007).

Group reading

Group reading can take many different forms and can serve different purposes. For teachers wanting to ensure they hear every child in the class read regularly, working with groups can be economical of their time. Group reading can also provide opportunities to teach aspects of literacy to children with similar needs. However, group reading can also be used as part of a literate classroom in which texts are discussed and shared, often with teachers and other adults, but sometimes just between children. For successful group reading, some simple resources will be needed:

- Multiple copies of books/poems, etc.
- Activity or discussion cards might be provided, especially where children work without an adult.
- Reference sources such as dictionaries, a thesaurus, atlases and internet access can help children to find information about aspects of the texts, such as location, meanings of words, historical context and whether stories are based on real events.

In this section, we explore some approaches to group reading and consider how they might help integrate children's literature into the classroom.

Guided reading

The National Strategies (DfES, 2006) advocated guided reading as a strategy. Typical guidance for teachers included:

- *Begin with the 'big picture'* – let the children see the whole text before you look at reading as the sentences and words within it with them.
- *Let them read independently at first* – they may read aloud as you monitor, 'structured eavesdropping'. You may follow their progress one at a time.
- *Ask questions about the content of the text* – this helps to give context to their 'guesses' and attempts at difficult words and phrases.
- *Ask about any phrases which puzzled them* – encourage other children to make suggestions: don't just tell them. Try to develop a sense of enquiry and an ability to work things out.
- *Ask about any words which puzzled them* – use context to determine meaning, use phonics to decide upon pronunciation. Relate the new to the familiar.
- *Develop understanding through extrapolation* – write down some of the words and phrases and consider how they might be used in other contexts.
- *Consider re-reading the text as a group* – encourage turn-taking and close following of text. While this approach was advocated as a possible development, the National Strategies were keen to emphasise that the main approach to guided reading should not be taking turns to read around the group.

Waugh and Jolliffe (2017) identify classroom management strategies for guided reading:

- Always sit in a position that allows you to scan the whole class from time to time.
- Occasionally make it clear that you are aware of what children are doing.
- Praise those who are getting on quietly.
- Resist the temptation to leave your group to help others.
- Try to create a climate of independence in which children are praised for having a go at solving problems without constant recourse to the teacher.

In a report aimed at English subject leaders, but also at trainee teachers and newly qualified teachers, Oxford School Improvement summed up the value of regular guided reading as helping to broaden children's reading experience by

> '... giving them access to the language of books and literature, and helping them to form opinions about books and authors. A carefully-selected text will be one that children are able to read reasonably confidently but which also provides an appropriate challenge in terms of language and subject matter' (2017: 10).

Reading around the group

This approach can include some of the strategies used in guided reading, such as discussing content, phrases and words, and making teaching points about spelling and grammar. However, if children's turns involve, say, reading a page each, there can be a tendency for them not to follow and to lose track when their turn ends. Some teachers have developed other ways of ensuring turn-taking without children losing concentration. For example, children might be assigned roles to play, including as characters in stories who speak the dialogue, while others might read the rest of the text, including things like 'said John nervously', 'she screamed in terror' and 'whispered the mermaid'. By focusing on the presentation, children can embed their understanding of the punctuation of direct speech, as well as responding to the verbs and adverbs which tell them how to deliver their lines.

Groups reading and preparing to read to others

One of the challenges for teachers of working with a single group is what to do with the rest of the class. One solution is to train them to use group reading techniques independently. This might mean having mixed ability groups so that there are children who can help when others struggle, and it can be a good way of making reading purposeful, especially when groups are asked to read something together in preparation for presenting it to the rest of the class. They might read an exciting section or an interesting piece of dialogue, or could read, learn and perform a poem, for example.

Groups discussing texts

Book clubs are popular among some adults and often involve a social gathering with refreshments. Approaches vary, but often everyone agrees in advance to read the same book and to come along prepared to discuss it. (A similar format is the basis for BBC Radio 4's *A Good Read*, except that each of the panellists reads their own and everyone else's recommendation.) In the classroom, a special area, such as a reading corner, might be used to make the 'book club' feel special and you might even provide refreshments to be enjoyed during discussions. Children might be given the task of producing lists of strengths and weaknesses of books or a blurb to promote it. They could find extracts to read to the class to whet people's appetites for reading it.

This chapter has examined the reading environment and how this can be enhanced through engaging the interest of children and other adults. Many of the examples and suggested strategies cost little or nothing and their success will depend upon the enthusiasm and commitment which teachers can generate. In the next chapter, we will look at ways in which children's literature can be incorporated into the curriculum so that it is an integral part of teaching and learning.

Learning outcomes review

By reading this chapter, you have considered:

- The physical environment of the classroom and the school and how it can be developed to ensure children's literature is valued
- Strategies to promote reading for pleasure and the development of reading skills
- Ways in which children can take ownership of areas of the classroom and school to ensure that reading is valued
- How other adults can support children's reading development and engagement with children's literature

Questions for discussion

- What could you do to make your classroom into a better environment for reading?
- What factors in your classroom and among your pupils might affect the success of group reading activities?
- How could you get other adults more involved in supporting your pupils' reading?
- How could the library facilities in your classroom and your school be made more appealing?

For your bookshelf

Morpurgo, M. (2004) *Private Peaceful.* London: HarperCollins.
This story evokes clearly and beautifully both rural life before the Great War, and life in the trenches for the innocent soldiers who went to fight. Some sensitive and adult themes make it suitable only for the top end of the primary age-range.

Further reading

Jolliffe, W. (2007) *Cooperative Learning in the Classroom: Putting it into Practice.* London: Paul Chapman. This book provides a rationale for cooperative learning and lots of practical ideas and techniques.

Just Imagine Story Centre (www.justimaginestorycentre.co.uk) and BookTrust (www.booktrust.org.uk) are excellent at providing information about new and established texts. Both websites include book reviews, author interviews, lesson ideas, and top tips for teachers to use when selecting and working with texts in the classroom.

Who Next Children's Author Guide (www.whonextguide.com). As the website states: 'Writers of children's fiction are listed with suggestions of other authors who write in a similar way, together with key book and series titles.'

The Open University Reading for Pleasure website (www.researchrichpedagogies.org) is packed with ideas and research, as well as examples of classroom practice.

References

Brown, P. (2021) Building a virtual classroom, *Education Today,* March: 30–32.
Cremin, T., Mottram, M., Powell, S., Collins, R. and Safford, K. (2014) *Building Communities of Engaged Readers: Reading for Pleasure.* London: Routledge.
Crew, M. (2021) *Literature Review on the Impact of COVID-19 on Families, and Implications for the Home Learning Environment.* London: National Literacy Trust. Available at: https://cdn.literacytrust.org.uk/media/documents/Updated_COVID-19_Literature_Review.pdf (accessed 25 August 2021).
Department for Education (DfE) (2011) *Teachers' Standards: Guidance for school leaders, school staff and governing bodies* (updated 2013 and 2021). London: DfE. Available at: https://www.gov.uk/government/publications/teachers-standards (accessed 15 February 2022).
Department for Education (DfE) (2013) *The National Curriculum in England: Key Stages 1 and 2 framework document.* London: DfE. Available at: https://www.gov.uk/government/publications/national-curriculum-in-england-primary-curriculum (accessed 30 July 2021).
Department for Education (DfE) (2021) *The Reading Framework: Teaching the foundations of literacy.* London: DfE. Available at: https://assets.publishing.service.gov.uk/government/uploads/system/uploads/attachment_data/file/1000986/Reading_framework_Teaching_the_foundations_of_literacy_-_July-2021.pdf (accessed 12 July 2021).

Department for Education and Skills (DfES) (2006) *Primary Framework for Literacy and Mathematics*. London: DfES.

Desforges, C. with Abouchaar, A. (2003). *The Impact of Parental Involvement, Parental Support and Family Education on Pupil Achievements and Adjustment: A literature review*. Research Report #RR433. Nottingham: DfES. Available at: https://dera.ioe.ac.uk/6305/ (accessed 15 February 2022).

Jolliffe, W. (2007) *Cooperative Learning in the Classroom: Putting it into Practice*. London: Paul Chapman.

Mat Roni, S. and Merga, M.K. (2019) The influence of extrinsic and intrinsic variables on children's reading frequency and attitudes: An exploration using an artificial neural-network, *Australian Journal of Education*, 63 (3): 270–291.

Ofsted (2006) *Good School Libraries: Making a difference to learning*. Available at: https://dera.ioe.ac.uk/5792/1/Good%20school%20libraries%20making%20a%20difference%20to%20learning%20%28PDF%20format%29.pdf (accessed 15 February 2022).

Oxford School Improvement (2017) *Teaching the Reading Curriculum: The role of high-quality guided reading*. Available at: https://cdn.oxfordowl.co.uk/2017/04/25/13/25/23/885/bp_osi_teachingreading.pdf (accessed 16 August 2021).

Teravainen, A. and Clark. C. (2017) *School Libraries: A literature review of current provision and evidence of impact*. London: National Literacy Trust. Available at: https://cdn.literacytrust.org.uk/media/documents/2017_06_30_free_research_-_school_library_review_XxR5qcv.pdf (accessed 15 February 2022).

Waugh, D. and Jolliffe, W. (2017) *English 5–11: A Guide for Teachers*, 3rd edition. London: Routledge.

Williams, A. (2021) *Get Everyone Reading*. Swindon: School Library Association. Available at: https://www.sla.org.uk/get-everyone-reading (accessed 16 August 2021).

3 Children's literature across the curriculum

Learning outcomes

By reading this chapter, you will:

- Consider how we can use stories, poems and song lyrics, as well as non-fiction texts, to enhance teaching and learning across the curriculum
- See examples of teachers incorporating children's literature into work across the curriculum
- Discover examples of stories and poems which might be incorporated into a range of curricular areas

Link to the Teachers' Standards

3. Demonstrate good subject and curriculum knowledge

- have a secure knowledge of the relevant subject(s) and curriculum areas, foster and maintain pupils' interest in the subject, and address misunderstandings

4. Plan and teach well structured lessons

- impart knowledge and develop understanding through effective use of lesson time
- promote a love of learning and children's intellectual curiosity
- contribute to the design and provision of an engaging curriculum within the relevant subject area(s)

(DfE, 2011: 11)

Link to the National Curriculum

6.3 Teachers should develop pupils' reading and writing in all subjects to support their acquisition of knowledge. Pupils should be taught to read fluently, understand extended prose (both fiction and non-fiction) and be encouraged to read for pleasure.

(DfE, 2013: 10)

> Good comprehension draws from linguistic knowledge (in particular of vocabulary and grammar) and on knowledge of the world. Comprehension skills develop through pupils' experience of high-quality discussion with the teacher, as well as from reading and discussing a range of stories, poems and non-fiction. All pupils must be encouraged to read widely across both fiction and non-fiction to develop their knowledge of themselves and the world in which they live, to establish an appreciation and love of reading, and to gain knowledge across the curriculum.
>
> (DfE, 2013: 14)

One of the reasons frequently heard for teachers not spending time sharing fiction with their pupils is that the curriculum is so vast and demanding that there isn't time in the school day for reading to classes. In this chapter, you will read about how two teachers developed a cross-curricular topic to include an educational visit and studies in a range of subject areas, drawing upon appropriate children's literature to enhance understanding and develop interest and curiosity. You will also see how children's literature can enhance learning in many areas across the curriculum and help engage children with concepts in subjects such as history, science, geography and mathematics. You will discover as well that you can enhance your own subject knowledge and understanding of topics through children's literature, as the research focus on science later in this chapter demonstrates.

The following case study shows how two teachers developed a theme for their year-group to study, and extended it across the curriculum for half a term's topic work, after introducing an element of the topic through a children's novel.

Case study: Developing a theme using children's literature as a stimulus

Maeve and Sadiq taught the two Year 5 classes in a suburban school in West Durham. They planned a summer term project focused on the east coast, because many of the children had never visited the seaside and the teachers felt there were opportunities for cross-curricular studies. They spent time online and then a weekend exploring the area for potential places of interest to visit. With uncertainty about possible lockdowns and limited availability of inexpensive hotels, Maeve and Sadiq decided that they would arrange day trips rather than a longer residential visit. They felt that an advantage of this would be the opportunity to visit places that were within reach of the school but not close to each other. Therefore, they planned trips to Bamburgh in Northumberland and Souter Lighthouse near Sunderland.

They prepared materials which would cover different curriculum areas: the changing face of the landscape due to coastal erosion for geography; the local history of the fishing trade and the development of shipping; and the various stories of lighthouses, especially down the east coast of Britain. In particular, they wanted children to learn about Grace Darling, whose heroic deeds were commemorated in Bamburgh.

Sadiq and Maeve introduced the topic by asking the children questions, to find out what they knew about their nearby coastline. Working from the children's own ideas and suggestions, they constructed a 'KWL chart' with different topic areas, including History, Fishing, Shipping, Seaside holidays, Wildlife and so on, with three columns – What we Know (K), What we Want to know (W) and What we have Learnt (L) – for each topic. The chart was displayed on the wall so that the last column could be filled in as the study progressed.

Literature, of course, doesn't only apply to fiction. Teaching children to research by reading and interpreting factual information is a valuable exercise. Sadiq and Maeve made a collection of brochures, websites, tide timetable, maps, pictures and other information about the area they wanted to study, and showed these to the classes, explaining how each was used. They also wanted to incorporate stories, poems and songs to bring the topic to life. They needed to factor in the possibility that trips would be called off due to the pandemic and so they gathered weblinks, texts and video materials that could be used for virtual visits if necessary. They also considered how they could deliver the topic to children who were being home educated.

Sadiq and Maeve wanted to explore the nature of heroism with the children and consider how heroic deeds and heroic role models might influence us. They decided to draw upon the book which Maeve had read to her previous class: *'Girls Can't Play Football!'* (Waugh, 2015) in which Lauren Morris tries to persuade boys at her school to take her footballing skills seriously. A turning point in the story is a chapter which features a school assembly.

> Assembly on Thursday was always the best of the week because Mr Long told the children a story after hymns and prayers. Sometimes the stories were made up, but often they were about people who had done great things. This time Mr Long began by asking a question.
>
> 'Can anyone tell me anything about Grace Darling?'
>
> 'Is it a bird, sir?'
>
> 'No, Richard Bell, not *grey starling* ... Grace Darling!' Mr Long said the name again more slowly.
>
> Some of the Y6 children giggled when they heard the name Darling, but Mr Long silenced them with a frown. 'Yes, it is a funny name,' he said, 'but it's the name of one of the bravest people who ever lived. Lauren Morris ...'
>
> Lauren was startled at hearing her name. She looked up and felt her cheeks flushing as they had at the football game the night before.
>
> 'Come out here, please Lauren,' said Mr Long. Lauren had not been talking and she had not done anything to get into trouble. She hesitated for a moment, but Mr Long spoke again. 'Come on Lauren, I won't bite you. I just want you to help me with my story.'

> Lauren got up slowly and walked to the front of the hall. She could feel a hundred children's eyes upon her and she tried not to look at anyone.
>
> 'Now Lauren, I want you to hold this label so that everyone can read the name of the heroine of this story.' The Headteacher handed her a piece of card on which was written *Grace Darling*, and she held it in front of her as she faced the rest of the school.
>
> Mr Long told the story of how Grace and her father had left their lighthouse and had put to sea in a tiny rowing boat in stormy seas, and had rescued sailors from a ship called *The Forfarshire*. Mr Long told the story brilliantly and everyone in the hall listened carefully as he painted a picture with words, so that they could almost see the waves crashing over the boat and hear the wind howling.
>
> As she walked back to her place, Lauren ignored the boys who were smirking and whispering to each other. She held her head up and took no notice when Adam pointed at her and nudged Michael. Lauren had a plan and she was going to put it into action very soon.
>
> (Waugh 2015: 6–8)

In the following chapter we find the paragraph:

> Lauren had made up her mind. She was not going to *ask* the boys if she could play. She was going to *tell* them that she was playing. If Grace Darling had been brave enough to go out to sea in an open boat in a storm to rescue stranded sailors, Lauren Morris was not going to let a few silly boys frighten her.
>
> (Waugh 2015: 10–11)

This prompted a discussion which the two teachers had prepared for, asking:

- Why does the author include the story of Grace Darling in a story about a girl playing football?
- Who was Grace Darling and how can we find out?
- What was her life like?
- Why did she die so young?

They directed the class to the book *My Name is Grace Darling* (2019) by Geraldine Terry and Moira Pagan, which they could access through Kindle in the classrooms. Terry and Pagan's beautifully illustrated book is narrated as if by Grace herself and creates a picture of life for a child in a poor family in the early nineteenth century. From this and other online sources the children found portraits, pictures of memorials to Grace, and even images of a chocolate box brought out by Cadbury's to commemorate her heroism.

Maeve and Sadiq followed up by introducing the classes to other stories in the class libraries in which lighthouses feature: stories such as *The Lighthouse Keeper's Lunch* by Ronda and David Armitage, *Moominpappa at Sea* by Tove Jansson and *Marianne Dreams* by Catherine Storr. They introduced the poem *Flannan Isle*, which proved one of the most successful aspects of the project in the classroom. The discussion and investigation prompted by this poem *Flannan Isle*, which was written in 1912 by Wilfred Wilson Gibson and based upon the disappearance of three lighthouse keepers from the Flannan Lighthouse, northwest of Lewis in Scotland, in December 1900, captivated the children. They liked the eerie tone of the poem and its imagery. After reading the poem, they speculated on what might have happened to the men and were particularly intrigued by the verse:

> *Yet, as we crowded through the door,*
> *We only saw a table, spread*
> *For dinner, meat and cheese and bread;*
> *But, all untouched; and no one there:*
> *As though, when they sat down to eat,*
> *Ere they could even taste,*
> *Had risen and left the bread and meat:*
> *For at the table-head a chair*
> *Lay tumbled on the floor.*

After much discussion of this section and other parts of the poem, children were asked to find out more about the mystery to see if Gibson's poem provided a true reflection of events. The teachers provided materials from Twinkl (see Further Reading), which offer a more factual account accompanied by questions and answers. From these and various websites, children made notes and then shared their findings, concluding that much of the poem was based upon Gibson's imagination, but that it had some basis in facts. This led to a wider discussion about history and how we know about past events, and the possibility that in being passed down through generations, 'facts' might become distorted.

The teachers went on to play a YouTube clip of the rock band Genesis's song *The Mystery of the Flannan Isle Lighthouse* (1968), which focuses on the eeriness of the island, and this too prompted discussion about facts and fantasy.

Over the next few weeks, the following avenues were explored by the two classes:

- How old are lighthouses? The Pharos of Alexandria was one of the Seven Wonders of the ancient world – fire by night and smoke by day, for travellers across the sea.
- What would happen without them? The story of the Inchcape Rock (poem by Robert Southey).
- Where are lighthouses? A search with maps and atlases found lighthouses all around the coast, including two at Flamborough, a Roman one at Filey, and even one in the town centre at Withernsea, in East Yorkshire. Sites and shipping lanes were looked at.
- How far would the light travel?
- How did they build them on rocky sites? (The engineer John Smeaton rediscovered 'hydraulic lime', a form of concrete used by the Romans that will set under water.)

- Why are they that shape? Smeaton modelled his tower on the shape of an oak tree. The children used card and paper to construct towers of different shapes (cylinder, cuboid, cone and so on) and then, under supervision outdoors, turned a water hose on them to see which was the most resilient. They found that the conical shape stood up to the buffeting best.
- Why does everyone seem to like lighthouses? They're a symbol of safety and protection. The teachers introduced the song and hand motion video, 'My Lighthouse' (https://www.youtube.com/watch?v=JeJvKkBV6rY), which the children enjoyed learning and performing. Although the song has a suggestion of religious overtone, there is only one reference to 'My God' and they felt this was sufficiently non-specific to be acceptable in a multi-faith classroom.

The unit of work culminated in an assembly presented to the rest of the school.

This case study shows how, from the initial stimulus of a story, discussions about gender and heroism arose. When the topic was extended, a wide-ranging study of lighthouses and the coastline of the UK had spread into many areas of the curriculum and left the two classes with a deeper understanding of their own area and environment.

In the following section, you will find ideas for how you might augment teaching and learning through the use of literature, in a range of curriculum subjects.

Stories and poems which could enhance teaching and learning across the curriculum

Art

In *The Midnight Fox* by Betsy Byars, Tom, a boy from the city, spends the summer on his uncle's farm and discovers a fox and its cubs. One of the most appealing aspects of this tale is the flights of fantasy Tom has, including describing what it would be like to discover a colour no one has ever seen before. Reading this passage as a prelude to an art lesson involving colour mixing can set children an interesting challenge: can they create a new colour and can they remember how they did so? And what would they call it?

Geography

Geography at KS1 is largely concerned with learning to recognise and name physical features and become aware of the different regions and climates in the world, and there are many appealing books which will help with this. A good starting point might be *Oliver Who Travelled Far and Wide*, the story of Oliver's bedtime search for his lost teddy. This award-winning picture book by Mara Bergman, with a story told in rhyme, shows Oliver's travels on his toy train through deserts, rainforest, mountains and snowy forests looking for Ted. As he goes, we can see the different terrains (and pause to discuss them if we want to).

Geography offers great possibilities for cross-curricular work; different climates and the animals who live in them are often a source of great interest to young children. *Handa's Surprise*, the classic picture book by Eileen Browne, can show a great deal more than the story: what are the different fruits? What are the animals she meets? How is her friend's village different from our villages and towns? KS1 classes can soon learn the idea of lives, communities and climates different from ours.

For older children, a book like Michael Morpurgo's *Kensuke's Kingdom* can be a wonderful geography lesson as well as an exciting story. Michael and his family are sailing round the world in a small ship, when he is thrown off the ship by rough weather at night and cast up on a lonely island in the Pacific. There is the excitement of the voyage around the world, with the sealife encountered on the journey, the winds and currents of the oceans, and then the details and practicalities of life on a desert island. Classes can trace the journey on world maps, and add details of what was to be found in each place. The story is a page-turner, the research and detail are assiduous. At KS2 children should, in addition to knowing the seven oceans and five continents, be able to: 'identify the position and significance of latitude, longitude, Equator, Northern Hemisphere, Southern Hemisphere, the Tropics of Cancer and Capricorn, Arctic and Antarctic Circle, the Prime/Greenwich Meridian and time zones (including day and night)' (DfE, 2013: 186). This story teaches these topics without ever seeming to have a didactic purpose.

History

Stories set in a historical period, featuring characters that children can identify with, can create a strong understanding of life in a different age, and there is a wealth to choose from. Some periods have been written about extensively, and the nineteenth and twentieth centuries offer us both stories published at the time and those written later as deliberate reconstructions. We suggest below some titles which may help enhance appreciation of specific times which your class may be studying.

- For Tudor times, Alison Uttley's classic *A Traveller in Time* gives a lot of detail of farm and household life, in a story involved with Mary Queen of Scots and the Babington Plot.
- For older KS2 classes, Michael Morpurgo's *War Horse* and *Private Peaceful* both evoke the First World War and its impact on domestic farm life as well as on the battlefields.

- For the Second World War on the home front, there are several well-known classics showing life as an evacuee – *Carrie's War* by Nina Bawden and *The Lion and the Unicorn* by Shirley Hughes are both mentioned in more detail in Chapter 5, and *Goodnight Mr. Tom* by Michelle Magorian is another good starting point, which has also been made into a film.
- Although the focus of National Curriculum history is on British history, Laura Ingalls Wilder's Little House books give beautifully clear and detailed descriptions of, for instance, building a log cabin and the laying of the first railroad tracks in frontier America. Although the books are sometimes seen as controversial because of their references to the settling of the Osage lands in the West (this is discussed further in Chapter 7), the descriptions are excellent. These could be very useful when learning about life in pre-mechanised society.
- The Romans and Roman Britain are a frequent topic of interest to primary-aged children, and for studying these an excellent source is Caroline Lawrence's Roman Mysteries series. These fourteen books tell a linked story, though each is self-contained. A group of four children – a Roman girl, a Jewish boy, a Greek orphan who is mute, and a freed African slave-girl – travel around the ancient world, having adventures and solving puzzles and mysteries. The author's classical knowledge is sound and accurate, and unfamiliar words and terms are explained clearly without seeming oppressively didactic.

The following case study shows how one teacher used these books when leading a topic on the Romans.

Case study: Roman life

William's Year 5 class was studying Roman life in History. He wanted to help them develop a sense of the Romans as real people and families, so chose to read *The Thieves of Ostia* by Caroline Lawrence (the first book in the Roman Mysteries sequence) as a class reader. This book is set in Ostia, the ancient port of Rome, and within an exciting story gives a lot of detail about towns and town life, houses, and family life. The children were shocked and fascinated by the idea of slavery, and this led to a discussion on the topic – this tied in with work on human rights which they had been learning about in PSHE lessons. They used cardboard and plasticine to make 'wax' tablets, as described in the book, which are the mute boy's only way to communicate, They also particularly enjoyed the details of food and meals, and at the end of the topic had a 'Roman meal' together, reclining on cushions and trying such things as stuffed dates, bread with peppered goat's cheese, watermelon and chestnut pudding, although the more exotic dishes mentioned in the book (sea snails in their shells, for instance, and chopped sows' udders) were omitted. They tried their hand at arithmetic using Roman numerals, and agreed that the modern system was easier.

William felt that using the book to get a sense of everyday life had been effective and had helped acceptance of some ideas which seem strange to modern children, like praying to a variety of different gods or going to the public baths. He planned at the end of the module to be able to take the children to a good display of Roman artefacts, such as at the British Museum or the museum at Vindolanda on Hadrian's Wall, but knew that old things in glass cases are never as evocative as when one can actually understand their role in everyday life.

Mathematics

MathsThroughStories.org is a non-profit and research-based initiative, based at the University of Reading's Institute of Education. It sets out to help mathematics learners around the world develop their conceptual understanding in mathematics, and to help them foster positive attitudes towards the subject through the power of storytelling. The publications of this group, by a range of authors, include the American series of *Charlesbridge Math Adventures*. More than 500 titles are available on the website, covering topics from multiplication and fractions to probability and the role of zero (who is lonely because he can't play Addemup with all the other digits) in entertaining stories. Many of the stories have a linking theme; for example, a mystery or problem that is solved by mathematical skills. Children are shown how mathematical ideas can be helpful in life, as well as understanding the terminology.

Of course, it is not suggested that reading these books will replace maths lessons, but they can prove an excellent replacement for 'one more worksheet', and could prove a valuable resource both for extension work and for explaining ideas to children who have difficulty with abstract concepts. The MathsThroughStories website also offers teaching ideas and materials, and is well worth a visit.

Furner (2018: 6) describes *A Cloak for the Dreamer* by Aileen Friedman and Kim Howard as 'a wonderful story to read to students to teach about two-dimensional geometry, spatial sense, and tessellations'. A tailor asks his three sons each to make a cloak for the Archduke's journey. Two use rectangles and triangles to create beautiful coloured cloaks, while the youngest uses circles which look beautiful but do not make a cloak which will keep the Archduke warm because they don't tessellate. The boy doesn't want to be a tailor, but wishes to travel, so his family secretly cut the circles of cloth into hexagons and restitch them to provide him with a cloak for his travels.

You can find a presentation read by a teacher during lockdown in the USA on YouTube (https://www.youtube.com/watch?v=RX5XLP737OA).

Research focus: Reading for pleasure, and attainment in maths, vocabulary and spelling

The 1970 British Cohort Study (BCS70) follows the lives of a nationally representative sample of 6,000 people born in England, Scotland and Wales in a single week of 1970. Every few years members of the cohort are interviewed about various aspects of their lives, from education and employment to physical and mental health. Among their key findings reported in 2014, Sullivan and Brown found that 'Reading for pleasure had a powerful influence on children's learning, especially for the development of their vocabularies, but also for their spelling and mathematics skills' (2014: 1). Participants who 'read books often at age 10 and more than once a week at age 16 gained higher test results at age 16 than those who read less regularly. In other words, reading for pleasure was linked to greater intellectual progress, both for vocabulary, spelling and mathematics' (2014: 1).

The study concluded that reading for pleasure made a difference to children's progress which was 'around four times greater than the difference made by having a parent with a degree'. Because reading introduces new vocabulary and ideas, readers were better able to 'understand and absorb new information and concepts across the curriculum' (2014: 3).

For a detailed analysis, see Sullivan and Brown (2015).

Activity

Consider the following:

Why might reading for pleasure improve people's vocabulary and spelling?
Why might reading for pleasure improve progress in mathematics?

Physical education

From Head to Toe by Eric Carle is a colourful book to share with young children, illustrated in Carle's usual collage style, in which readers are invited to join in with simple movements shown them by animals. It's a good way to conduct a quick classroom workout when space and time might be limited.

Music

Activity

Think of songs or hymns you sang in school. Did you ever find you were singing words you didn't understand, but joined in with anyway? Even those which seem obvious to adults – 'no crying he makes', from *Away in a Manger*, perhaps, or 'when the grass is jewelled' from *Autumn Days* – can be baffling to young children. Most schools no longer present children with hymns containing lines like 'all laud we would render' or 'Say, shall we yield thee in costly oblation' (both lines from hymns popular in primary schools for many years), but it's still all too possible for singing to take place without understanding.

Every time you have a singing session, in class or in assembly, you're looking at literature. Children are no longer expected to learn or to know complicated hymns with convoluted and archaic lyrics – but every song is a poem of some kind. Take time to look at the lyrics; explain unfamiliar words, look at patterns of rhythm and rhyme to show how the words fit the music. You and your class will enjoy a song more if you all appreciate what's going on in it. Singing together also gives your class a chance to think about performance and presentation (see the Statutory Requirements for poetry at the head of chapter).

Science

Science in fiction written for children is still a thinly populated area. Science fiction, such as the books of Nicholas Fisk, introduces some ideas which may spark the imagination, and should be available in the class library for KS2 pupils, but are a long way from anything likely to be met in the classroom.

Science can be supported by literature through any book which encourages children to ask the right kind of questions. Most people will have seen how a small child goes through a stage where everything is greeted with 'Why?' The job of science is to keep asking this, and learning how to find the answers that will give us a better understanding of the world. One book that shows how this can work is *The Diary of Curious Cuthbert*, by Jack Challoner: Cuthbert lives in a land where the people in his village are all getting ill, and wants to find out why. The story is told in a verse diary form, but includes scientific details about, for instance, how microbes cause disease and how we can use scientific equipment to help learning.

George's Secret Key to the Universe is a novel by Lucy Hawking with her father Stephen, set in the perennially interesting topic of the planets and the solar system: it's a good read and contains sound factual sections explaining the ideas and vocabulary of the subject. The book explains such things as the movement of the planets and the way the earth's rotation gives us day and night, while the hero has to be rescued from a black hole … it would fit well into study of the solar system.

In 1989, Russell Stannard, Emeritus Professor of Physics at the Open University, launched his Uncle Albert series with *The Time and Space of Uncle Albert*, which set out ambitiously to explain the Theory of Special Relativity to young readers. Uncle Albert takes his niece Gedanken on a series of adventures, which involve tasks such as trying to catch up with a light beam. There is humour as well as science in the stories, and all the reasoning is clearly explained, but they could be a conceptually challenging read.

Research focus: Teaching nature of science through children's literature

A study by Akerson et al. (2019) in the USA found that pre-service early childhood teachers who created picture books for their pupils to teach about the nature of science (NOS) developed their own scientific understanding by doing so. They concluded: 'Incorporating children's literature and reflective writing seems a powerful tool for teaching about NOS to early childhood teachers, and to portray NOS to early childhood students' (2019: 2781–2782).

Mahzoon-Hagheghi et al. (2018), in a study in Texas, found similar benefits where teachers taught literacy and nature of science together. They also concluded: 'The use of science-themed children's literature can improve the understanding of science concepts in the classroom' (2018: 47).

Food technology

There are many books for younger children on the topic of healthy eating and food preparation. *Oliver's Vegetables* by Vivian French tells the story of how picky Oliver is persuaded to try vegetables other than chips through spending time in the garden with his grandpa. Aisha Saeed's *Bilal Cooks Daal* shows how Bilal introduces his friends to the long, slow preparation of a healthy and delicious dish. The book is brightly and appealingly presented, and contains a recipe at the end which could be prepared at home for the children to try. (First published in the USA, the book does contain the unfamiliar name cilantro for the herb we know as coriander, but this is no obstacle.) Perhaps the classic in this field is Lauren Child's *I Will Never Not Ever Eat a Tomato*, in which fussy and stubborn Lola is tricked into enjoying a wider variety of food.

English

We have left English until last, because the twin subjects of language and literature are closely linked at every level in our English curriculum. From everything they read or have read to them, children increase their knowledge and understanding of the English language and the ways we can use it to learn, excite, enthral or charm us. They can learn the appeal of using unusual vocabulary, or phrases that are unexpected and interesting. Looking at rhymes enhances understanding of phonemes in the language, and of how the same sound can be written in many different ways.

Nominative determinism is an interesting concept which children often enjoy – looking at the names of characters in books and spotting why they might have been chosen. From Roger Hargreaves' *Mr Men* series, through

Dahl's Miss Honey and Miss Trunchbull (in *Matilda*), to Hufflepuff and Slytherin Houses in the *Harry Potter* books, it's an idea used very widely in literature that characters' names can suggest what kind of person they are. You can introduce Dickens' schoolmaster Mr. Gradgrind (from *Hard Times*) or the domineering James Steerforth (in *David Copperfield*) – what does one expect from the name? Children can experiment with language, using their vocabulary to make up names which suggest the personalities of characters.

In the next chapter, we will look at ways in which children's literature can help us to explore personal characteristics and issues in more depth.

Learning outcomes review

By reading this chapter, you have:

- Considered how we can use stories, poems and song lyrics, as well as non-fiction texts, to enhance teaching and learning in many areas across the curriculum
- Seen examples of teachers incorporating children's literature into work across the curriculum
- Discovered examples of stories and poems which might be incorporated into a range of curricular areas

Questions for discussion

- Consider some of the topic areas you teach in different curricular areas. How could children's literature be used to enhance children's learning?
- Is it important to help children to distinguish between fact and fiction when they read stories and poems related to curriculum subjects? If so, how can you do this?

For your bookshelf

Armitage, R. and Armitage, D. (1977) *The Lighthouse Keeper's Lunch*. London: Scholastic.
For KS1, a humorous illustrated story of how the lighthouse keeper, Mr Grinling, has to constantly battle hungry seagulls to get his lunch safely delivered.

Jansson, T. (1965) *Moominpappa at Sea*. London: Puffin.
One story in a well-loved classic series. The Moomin family find themselves living in a strange lighthouse, where the tide constantly foils their attempts to make it homely.

Storr, C. (1958) *Marianne Dreams*. London: Faber & Faber.
What Marianne draws in the daytime, she dreams at night. As things get scary, she draws a lighthouse in the distance as a safe place to escape to. An unforgettable story.

Bibliography

Bawden, N. (1973) *Carrie's War*. London: Puffin.
Bergman, M. (2009) *Oliver Who Travelled Far and Wide*. London: Hodder Children's Books.
Browne, E. (2008) *Handa's Surprise*. London: Walker Books.
Byars, B. (1968) *The Midnight Fox*. New York: Scholastic.
Carle, E. (1997) *From Head To Toe*. New York: HarperCollins.
Challoner, J. (2017) *The Diary of Curious Cuthbert*. Bristol: Explaining Science Publishing.
Child, L. (2000) *I Will Never Not Ever Eat a Tomato*. Somerville, MA: Candlewick Press.
Dahl, R. (1988) *Matilda*. London: Jonathan Cape.
Dickens, C. (1849) *David Copperfield*. London: Bradbury & Evans.
Dickens, C. (1854) *Hard Times*. London: Bradbury & Evans.
French, V. (1995) *Oliver's Vegetables*. London: Hodder Children's Books.
Friedman, A. and Howard, K. (1994) *A Cloak for the Dreamer*. Leamington Spa: Scholastic.
Hawking, L. and Hawking, S. (2007) *George's Secret Key to the Universe*. London: Doubleday.
Hughes, S. (1998) *The Lion and the Unicorn*. London: Red Fox.
Lawrence, C. (2001) *The Thieves of Ostia*. London: Orion Children's Books.
Magorian, M. (1981) *Goodnight Mr. Tom*. London: Kestrel Books.
Morpurgo, M. (1982) *War Horse*. London: Kaye & Ward.
Morpurgo, M. (1999) *Kensuke's Kingdom*. London: Egmont.
Morpurgo, M. (2003) *Private Peaceful*. London: HarperCollins.
Saeed, A. (2019) *Bilal Cooks Daal*. New York: Salaam Reads.
Stannard, R. (1989) *The Time and Space of Uncle Albert*. London: Faber & Faber.
Uttley, A. (1939) *A Traveller in Time*. London: Faber & Faber.

Further reading

For Grace Darling Museum:
Museum factsheet, including a version for the visually impaired
Museum education pack with activities
https://rnli.org/find-my-nearest/museums/grace-darling-museum?utm_source=various&utm_medium=vanity_url&utm_campaign=museum_page&utm_content=gracedarling

For Bamburgh Castle:
The enigma of Bamburgh war hero revealed in new audio presentation
https://www.bamburghcastle.com/the-enigma-of-bamburghs-naval-war-hero/

For *The Mystery of Flannan Isle* resource pack, see Twinkl:
https://www.twinkl.co.uk/resource/t2-e-3013-the-mystery-of-flannan-isle-resource-pack

References

Akerson, V.L., Erumit, B.A. and Kaynak, N.E. (2019) Teaching Nature of Science through children's literature: An early childhood preservice teacher study, *International Journal of Science Education*, 41 (18): 2765–2787.

Department for Education (DfE) (2011) *Teachers' Standards: Guidance for school leaders, school staff and governing bodies* (updated 2013 and 2021). London: DfE. Available at: https://www.gov.uk/government/publications/teachers-standards (accessed 16 February 2022).

Department for Education (DfE) (2013) *The National Curriculum in England: Key Stages 1 and 2 framework document*. London: DfE. Available at: https://www.gov.uk/government/publications/national-curriculum-in-england-primary-curriculum (accessed 30 July 2021).

Furner, J.M. (2018) Using children's literature to teach mathematics: An effective vehicle in a STEM world, *European Journal of STEM Education*, 3 (3): 14. Available at: https://doi.org/10.20897/ejsteme/3874 (accessed 16 February 2022).

Genesis (1968) *The Mystery of the Flannan Isle Lighthouse* [demo]. Available at: https://www.youtube.com/watch?v=zauTs0VfI2o&list=RDzauTs0VfI2o&index=1 (accessed 23 August 2021).

Mahzoon-Hagheghi, M., Yebra, R., Johnson, R.D. and Sohn, L.N. (2018) Fostering a greater understanding of science in the classroom through children's literature, *Texas Journal of Literacy Education*, 6 (1): 41–50. Available at: https://eric.ed.gov/?id=EJ1183979 (accessed 16 February 2022).

Sullivan, A. and Brown, M. (2014) *Reading for Pleasure, and Attainment in Maths, Vocabulary and Spelling*. Institute of Education Research Briefing #106. London: Institute of Education. Available at: https://discovery.ucl.ac.uk/id/eprint/10018836/1/RB106_Reading_for_Pleasure_Sullivan.pdf (accessed 16 February 2022).

Sullivan, A. and Brown, M. (2015) Reading for pleasure and progress in vocabulary and mathematics, *British Educational Research Journal*, 41 (6): 971–991.

Terry, G. and Pagan, M. (2019) *My Name is Grace Darling*. Kindle edition. UK: Independent Publishing Network.

Waugh, D. (2015) *'Girls Can't Play Football!'*. Bishop's Castle: Constance Books.

4 Children's literature and Personal, Social and Health Education (PSHE)

Learning outcomes

By reading this chapter, you will be able to think about:

- The importance of developing empathy with characters in fiction and their situations
- Ways of exploring other lives
- The inclusion agenda and how differences can be both understood and celebrated
- Gender and children's literature

Link to the Teachers' Standards

5. Adapt teaching to respond to the strengths and needs of all pupils

- have a secure understanding of how a range of factors can inhibit pupils' ability to learn, and how best to overcome these
- demonstrate an awareness of the physical, social and intellectual development of children, and know how to adapt teaching to support pupils' education at different stages of development
- have a clear understanding of the needs of all pupils, including those with special educational needs; those of high ability; those with English as an additional language; those with disabilities; and be able to use and evaluate distinctive teaching approaches to engage and support them

8. Fulfil wider professional responsibilities

- develop effective professional relationships with colleagues, knowing how and when to draw on advice and specialist support
- take responsibility for improving teaching through appropriate professional development, responding to advice and feedback from colleagues
- communicate effectively with parents with regard to pupils' achievements and well-being

(DfE, 2011: 11–13)

Link to the curriculum

Relationships Education (Primary)

54. The focus in primary school should be on teaching the fundamental building blocks and characteristics of positive relationships, with particular reference to friendships, family relationships, and relationships with other children and with adults.

55. This starts with pupils being taught about what a relationship is, what friendship is, what family means and who the people are who can support them.

(DfE, 2019: 19)

National Curriculum

Through reading in particular, pupils have a chance to develop culturally, emotionally, intellectually, socially and spiritually. Literature, especially, plays a key role in such development.

(DfE, 2013: 13)

In this chapter, we shall look at how choice of reading in your classroom can enhance the discussion of PSHE and citizenship issues such as relationships, mental health and the environment, as well as looking specifically at two of the key issues which arise in the context of inclusion: physical disabilities and differences, and gender identity. Both of these are important areas and useful to consider alongside, and as part of, a PSHE curriculum. The American writer Rudine Sims Bishop coined the image of books as 'mirrors, windows or sliding glass doors' to refer to the different ways we can react with other lives presented through fiction (1990: 6). A mirror shows us something familiar; a window enables us to look at another kind of experience; sliding glass doors make it possible to share that experience more closely and develop a deeper understanding.

Just as it is often said that 'every teacher is a teacher of reading', so perhaps it is true to say that on some level 'every book gives some lesson in PSHE'. Books, or perhaps one should say story books, are usually about relationships, which may go wrong or bring happiness; about choices of behaviour, which may bring good or bad results; about external events and how one reacts to them; about human situations and responses. In children's books, the ideas are usually more explicit, but even in most adult literature there are, to use the old-fashioned term, morals to be found. As the Duchess says to Alice in *Alice's Adventures in Wonderland*, 'Everything's got a moral, if only you can find it'.

Activity

Think of the last few books you have read – either children's books in school, or in your own personal reading, assuming that your personal choice is not exclusively scientific textbooks or mathematical treatises. Write a list of four or five, and then make a note of what useful lesson you might learn from each. Whether it's 'Crime does not pay', 'Families should stick together', 'Friendship is important' or 'Don't take needless risks', we hope you will have found something worth sharing in your choices.

If you included some children's books, was the exercise easier with those?

Most schools have only a very limited spot in the week's timetable designated specifically for PSHE, and may struggle to fulfil the Secretary of State's edict that Relationships Education should be compulsory in all primary schools in England (DfE, 2019: 4). The guidance document refers to children's experiences 'growing up in an increasingly complex world and living their lives seamlessly on and offline', and comments that, 'This presents many positive and exciting opportunities, but also challenges and risks. In this environment, children and young people need to know how to be safe and healthy, and how to manage their academic, personal and social lives in a positive way' (DfE, 2019: 4).

Many books are available for readers from the very youngest of Reception classes onwards which can lead usefully into discussion of issues that will develop children's consciousness of each other and of the world around them. In this way, we can meet the DfE's requirements through the use of literature.

Research focus: Inference-generating questions

Kispal (2008: 30–31) describes how Narvaez (2002: 167) produced inference-generating questions for older second language learners, which could be asked in relation to narrative and expository texts. Some of those which relate to narratives with a moral theme typify Narvaez's approach:

> 1. Assist students' awareness that some demands in a story may conflict with others, e.g. by asking: *What was the problem? What was the worst thing the character faced? Were there differences in what the characters wanted?*
> 2. Increase students' moral sensitivity to the configuration of the situation. *What was going on? Who was thinking about what was going on? Who could be affected? Who was affected?*
> 3. Help students reason about possible actions. *What could be done? What would happen if? How might people react?'*
>
> (Kispal, 2008: 31)

Kispal points out that although the questions were designed for second language learners, they also represented 'good practice in mainstream literacy work, especially in upper Key Stage 2 and Key Stage 3'.

Activity

Before continuing, consider a piece of children's literature and see how Narvaez's inference-generating questions might be applied to it.

There are lively and colourful picture books about making friends, such as *Together We Can* by Caryl Hart, in which a simple rhyming text shows all kinds of ways in which people can interact in friendship. For the same age group, *The Blue Giant*, by Katie Cottle, introduces the idea of ocean pollution and the importance of clean seas and beaches, as Meera and her mother find plastic and debris deep in the ocean. Julian Lennon's *Touch the Earth* trilogy has an 'interactive button' to press on each page, as the reader flies round the world seeing and remedying environment problems. And Dr. Seuss's *The Lorax* pits biodiversity against environmental exploitation and capitalism through a fantastical landscape and a lively rhyming text ('Unless someone like you cares a whole awful lot, Nothing is going to get better. It's not'). Small children can even be introduced to the idea of mindfulness through books such as *Kaya's Heart Song*, by Diwa Tharan Sanders and Nerina Canzi, in which bright illustrations help tell the story of a small girl learning both to clear her mind and to undertake tasks in full awareness.

Research focus: Children developing understandings through engaging with a picture book

Braid and Finch (2015) studied how 9- and 10-year-old children responded when a picture book was read aloud in a small group setting in a New Zealand classroom. The book chosen was *Luke's Way of Looking*, by Nadia Wheatley, which is the story of a boy's unconventional artistic vision. The other boys in the class 'thought Luke was weird': the school and teacher are shown in a sepia palette, but Luke's visions and his paintings are brightly coloured. The study describes how the children 'used picture-book elements [*such as colour, shadow, light and shade*] to make meaning from text' (Braid and Finch, 2015: 120). Children were encouraged to respond to and discuss the story throughout the reading. The authors concluded that, 'Everything from the book's title to the endpapers and title pages convey meaning for readers to explore. The elements the illustrator uses in the pictures are clues for the reader to consider as they engage with the text as a whole' (2015: 121).

Braid and Finch stressed the importance of teachers' knowledge about how picture books work so that 'effective discussion and an in-depth literary understanding' (2015: 121) can be developed.

From this study we can see that picture books and graphic novels cannot be dismissed as the diet exclusively of pre-readers and small children: text and pictures can work together to enhance understanding and develop emotional engagement.

As readers progress from picture books to longer stories, it would be hard to find any text, from the Railway Children to Harry Potter, which does not carry messages about the strength of family and friendship and the importance of social behaviour. Victorian and Edwardian stories tended to lay the morality on thickly, with moralising magic creatures or authority figures; naughty children usually ended up penitent or dead. In more recent writing there is, thankfully, more understanding and room for ambivalence and acceptance, but there will be a point in just about any story you share with a class at which you could stop and say, 'Do you think he was right to do that?' or, 'Was she a good friend by doing that?'

In the current political climate, ecology is of ever-growing importance, and has in some ways become a topic of particular interest and concern to children and young people. There is a rapidly growing canon of factual and fiction books with ecological themes. *Song of the Dolphin Boy*, by Elizabeth Laird, has a strong story about saving dolphins from marine pollution, and also themes of social isolation and bullying. *Window*, by Jeannie Baker, is a wordless picture book, though not one aimed at small children: the book shows the ever-changing view through the same window as a baby grows to adulthood, and sends a strong message about urban development. The detailed pictures could give a great stimulus for children's writing.

The Reading Framework states that 'Children also need to learn about the lives of those whose experiences and perspectives differ from their own. Choosing stories and non-fiction that explore such differences begins to break down a sense of otherness that often leads to division and prejudice.' (DfE, 2021: 28). The idea that reading fiction shows us a way into other lives has been mentioned in Chapter 1. The representation in books of those whose lives are 'different' in ways other than outward circumstances is a sector which has grown enormously in recent years, as inclusion has become an increasingly important part of education.

Of the two broad areas we shall consider in this next part of the chapter, physical disability and gender identity, the first has been present in children's fiction for longer. In Victorian and Edwardian times, it was not uncommon to come across a physically disabled child in fiction, usually referred to in the language of the day as 'lame' or 'a cripple'. Such children were typically of a sweet and pious nature, and very often piously died towards *Pollyanna* the end of the book. Think of Dickens' Tiny Tim, or Beth in Alcott's *Little Women*. Other disabilities were very rarely encountered as, indeed, they would not have been familiar to the literate, middle-class child readership – those with any physical or mental abnormality would usually have been sequestered in special institutions, probably for their entire lives.

There were also the characters, usually girls, who suffered a serious illness or accident which led to their maturing and becoming an improved character. Susan Coolidge's Katy (in *What Katy Did*, 1911), Eleanor Porter's *Pollyanna* (1913), Johanna Spyri's Klara (in *Heidi*, 1880) and Frances Hodgson Burnett's Colin Craven in *The Secret Garden* (1911) are all examples of this phenomenon, where temporary disability turns out to be a wonderfully enriching experience. This idea persisted for a long time – it was common in children's fiction in the first half of the twentieth century for a reprehensible character to be reformed by some kind of near-death experience – and if their life was saved by the very person they had wronged or maligned, so much the better.

Thankfully, since the 1960s, writing about characters with a whole range of differences in ability has become much more common. At first there were books in which the disabled character was the plot device – the story being centred on how either this person as protagonist coped with life, or how their best friend learned to understand and help. A good example of this type of book is found in the work of Judy Blume, a leading American writer of the 1970s and 1980s. Blume covered many topics other writers at the time were not concerning themselves with – divorcing parents, menarche (the onset of menstruation for adolescent girls), a shoplifting friend, race, and religion. Her 1973 novel *Deenie* is narrated by a 13-year-old girl who develops scoliosis, and has to cope not only with the condition but also with her mother's reaction to it and her own attitude to accepting the situation. (The story is sensitively told, but has been banned in some US states because of an implicit reference to masturbation.)

An area which has grown greatly in recent years is the range of books for younger readers which explain or normalise physical problems. The semi-autobiographical graphic novel *El Deafo*, by Cece Bell, for instance, tells of the author's loss of hearing after contracting meningitis at the age of four, and not only explains her own situation in a lively and often humorous way, but gives valuable and clear description of how those around her can help make her understanding clearer. Cari Best's *My Three Best Friends and Me, Zulay*, also for a young readership, is the story of a blind girl in a mainstream school, who is determined to take an active part in Sports Day. Although these two books are by American authors, the stories and situations are universal, and both are available on YouTube and through Amazon and other online book sales.

Case study: Raising consciousness of different abilities and senses with a Year 3 class

Esther wanted to raise consciousness of different abilities and senses with her Year 3 class, and get them to appreciate the differences some people experience in their interpretation of the world. She began by considering sightedness. Most of the children had experience of such games as creeping up behind someone whose back was turned, or other games involving blindfolds. Most of them agreed that they didn't like being the blindfolded one, as it 'made them feel creepy' not to know who was near them.

The children then took part in various activities, including walking blindfolded from the back of the classroom to the door, identifying objects inside a bag by touch alone, and identifying other members of the class by voice alone while wearing blindfolds. The 'game' aspect of these engaged the children's interest, and provoked lively discussion afterwards of how they felt when they could not use their eyes. Esther then asked a series of questions, including:

- How many stairs are there in your house?
- What order are the spoons, forks and knives in, in your kitchen drawer?
- Does your back door open in or out?
- How many steps is it from your front door to the pavement outside?

Very few children knew all four answers. Esther pointed out that if they could not see, they would need to know all these things just to be able to get through a normal day.

She then asked the children, 'What do you think it would be like if you couldn't hear, as well as not being able to see?' Some of them had experience of older relations or grandparents with hearing loss, and were able to share their ideas. One boy had had grommets inserted when he was younger, and remembered slightly what it had been like before the operation, and not being able to understand what other children were saying. Most felt that you would not be able to do very much in life if you had either or both of these impairments.

Esther then introduced the book *The Story of Helen Keller: A Biography Book for New Readers* (by Christine Platt) to the class, and over the next sessions they read the story of the first deaf and blind woman to graduate from college and all that she eventually achieved.

Esther felt that the introductory activities had helped the children to think more deeply about what it would be like to have a sensory impairment, and enabled them to appreciate the situation more sensitively.

While the genre of fiction in which the disability is the story is still very much a growing range, there is also now an ever-increasing canon of books where one of the characters is otherly-abled in some way but this is an incidental aspect of the story – just as one character is tall, one has a pet dog, or perhaps one is mathematically gifted, so one may be a wheelchair user, partially sighted or autistic. For instance, in Caroline Lawrence's *Roman Mysteries* series (published from 2001 to 2009), one of the main protagonists is mute, and the central character in one book, *The Charioteer of Delphi*, has behaviour and speech patterns easily recognisable as being characteristic of children on the autism spectrum, although this is never referred to in the text. It is certainly becoming more common to have a leading character in a children's book who has some kind of physical disability, and this is a healthy step towards inclusiveness.

The area of gender identity and inclusiveness is one which has only relatively recently become something of relevance to the primary curriculum, and you may feel less confident in approaching this within your classroom. However, Relationships Education is a key factor in the KS1 and KS2 PSHE curriculum, and may touch on these issues; also, there may be children in your class whose home life and family circumstances have led them into contact with situations that might be regarded as unconventional: single-sex parents or gender fluidity, for instance. While some would suggest that detailed discussion of gender identity topics is not appropriate or helpful in the primary classroom, there are books for all age groups which can help approach these issues if you feel it is appropriate. It's a good idea always to discuss this with your management or team leader before going ahead though – the school may have specific policies or history in this area, or parents who may have concerns.

Activity

Think about the following nursery rhymes. What suggestions do they make about the roles of boys and girls?

Little Jack Horner
Little Miss Muffet
Georgy Porgy
Tom, Tom, the piper's son
Miss Polly had a dolly
Mary, Mary, quite contrary

Can you think of others which suggest certain behaviour is characteristic of boys or of girls?

Young children's perceptions of gender are reinforced by society from the moment a baby girl is given a pink teddy and a baby boy a blue one. Children learn gender roles from society, from the clothing and toys they are given, and from rhymes and stories. Think, for instance, of the endings of the 'classic' fairy stories and Disney films. Every girl needs a handsome prince! Although there are many alternative stories featuring non-stereotypical princesses, these are not usually met until later. Robinson and Jones Diaz cite a large body of research demonstrating that 'children have a strong sense of gender by age 3, and are actively constituting themselves as gendered subjects within rigid understandings of binary gender, and policing the gender performances of other children according to what they perceive to be "appropriate" masculine and feminine behaviour' (2005: 188). If you have seen, for instance, a bunch of little girls shooing a boy away from the home corner in a nursery, you will understand the broad truth of this. However, there are strong movements against the heteronormativity of society, and we can support this through the literature we choose in our classrooms. 'Normalising discourses of gender diminish the options and choices children have in their lives ... The construction of gender is about constructing social relationships that impact on us all' (Robinson and Jones Diaz, 2005: 212)

The history of LGBT+ literature for children has been controversial from the start. The earliest text to draw mass attention was *Jenny Lives with Eric and Martin* by Susanne Bösche, which was translated from Danish and appeared in English in 1983. The book told in words and photos the story of a young child's day, with nothing explicit: however, it attracted such opprobrium from the Press and from the Inner London Education Authority that it was banned from school libraries and became frequently cited as one of the factors influencing the Conservative administration's subsequent passing of the controversial Section 28 of the Local Government Act 1988, which forbade the promotion of homosexuality by local government.

There are books for very young children, which, while not overtly discussing gender issues, have themes of accepting and normalising differences. One well-known example is *And Tango Makes Three* by Justin Richardson and Peter Parnell, which tells the true story of two male penguins in a New York zoo who fall in love: the zookeeper sees this and gives them an egg from another nest, which Roy and Silo hatch and raise together. The book was originally aimed at 3- to 8-year-olds, though in some American public libraries it was later moved to adult shelves. The message and conclusion of the book is that happy families 'can look different'.

Another book which focuses on differences and confounding expectations is Michael Hall's *Red: A Crayon's Story*, in which a blue crayon whose label calls him Red is increasingly unhappy until he discovers his true identity. Gender issues are never specifically mentioned in the text, and the book could cover all kinds of identity situations or problems. The child, for instance, who is expected to be good at sport because she is tall, or expected to be good at mathematics because he is of Asian heritage, could find a message here about confounding stereotypes. There are various YouTube versions of this book available, as indeed there are of many of the books mentioned here, and you can find a useful range of teaching materials and activity suggestions at https://childrenslibrarylady.com/red-crayons-story/.

Girls' and boys' strong perception of their gender, and their different expectations of appropriate behaviour, strengthen as they get older and more socially aware of the pressure to conform. An example of how we can challenge these expectations can be found in the case study below.

Case study: Addressing gender stereotyping with Year 4

Des had found that the girls and boys in his class seldom mixed voluntarily or socialised outside the classroom, and tended to dislike it when asked to work together. He wanted to get his Year 4 class thinking about gender differences.

First he asked the children, working in pairs, to write down four statements which they could complete however they wished. The beginnings of the statements were:

- Girls are ...
- Boys are ...
- Girls always ...
- Boys always ...

The children shared their ideas first with their partner, and then with the class, and Des assembled them in four lists on the whiteboard. Fortunately, there was quite a lot of duplication of ideas, for instance of the ideas 'Boys are noisy' and 'Girls always giggle', so each column ended up with between six and eight statements instead of twelve in each. He then asked for a quick show of hands vote on whether the statements were true or false. The numbers in the class were thirteen boys and twelve girls, so the voting process would be fairly even, though slightly skewed towards the boys. The class enjoyed the voting; the boys tended enthusiastically to support the ideas which might be seen as negative about themselves (boys always shout too much, boys are messy) while the girls showed more resentment about negative ideas (girls always fuss with their hair, girls always cry).

Des then rubbed out the words 'Girls' and 'Boys' at the top of the board and swapped them around. He asked the class which statements they felt were still true. Nearly all were accepted as being true for both sides. 'Boys like frilly things' was rejected by all the boys, but 'Girls like frilly things', suggested by one of the boys, had also been fiercely disputed by the girls.

Next, Des asked the class if they felt girls and boys were treated differently in school – for instance, in the way that teachers spoke to them. One interesting point that emerged was that a teacher addressing a group of girls tended to use their names, but a group of boys was more often addressed as 'You lads!' or 'You boys!' He also asked whether those girls with brothers, and boys with sisters, found a difference between them and their siblings in what was expected of them at home – did they get asked to do different jobs? Did they feel their sister, or brother, 'got away with things' more? This brought several comments like, 'they never ask *him* to set the table' and '*she* never gets told off properly because she starts crying'.

Des thought it a good idea not to let this conversation go on too long, so he then told the class they were going to read a story which might make them think more about this kind of idea, and introduced *Bill's New Frock*.

The two best-known books about gender identity for the KS2 years are probably Anne Fine's *Bill's New Frock* and David Walliams' *The Boy in The Dress*. These are very different books, but both ones which are very likely to be found on the school bookshelf, so we shall include some discussion of them here. Both books contain a great deal of humour, which makes them popular reads; neither overtly discusses sexuality. In Anne Fine's book, Bill, who is perhaps 9 or 10 years old, simply wakes up to find he has become a girl, although his mindset is still very much that of a boy. The main thrust of the book comes from observations about how differently boys and girls are addressed and treated in school. There is no explanation of how or why the transformation has happened, and it miraculously reverses itself in the same way, to Bill's great relief. The book is a good launch for discussion of gender attitudes, and there are support materials available for classroom use: a resource book at https://shop.scholastic.co.uk/products/72994 and a digital resource at https://shop.scholastic.co.uk/products/78010.

Walliams' protagonist, Dennis, is slightly older at 12, and there is a hint that he may have been affected by the departure of his mother, leaving him in an all-male household. His liking for soft materials and pretty dresses leads him first to fashion magazines, then to friendship with a girl and to wearing dresses and makeup. After initial hostility and ridicule, Dennis is accepted and even imitated by his peers on the football team. His macho father and brother admire his courage and become closer to him. Even the 'headmaster with the heart of darkness' (Walliams, 2008: 162) who had expelled Dennis, is persuaded to reinstate him after being found dressed in female clothes himself. After the liberal acceptance of the rest of the book, it is slightly discordant that the persuasion is effected by the confrontation, 'What if it got out that you liked dressing like this? You'd be a laughing stock' (Walliams, 2008: 215). Thus the apparent message that cross-dressing is fine is countered by the idea that for an adult it is ridiculous and embarrassing. The book is much enjoyed by young readers, but perhaps too ambivalent to be taken seriously as a trail-blazing text for transvestism.

Some of the issues discussed may appear to have little relevance to many primary-aged children, but sensitively chosen literature can help them become more receptive to ideas of difference and bring awareness that there are many equally valid patterns for life.

The other big issue in inclusion, which has not so far been discussed, is race, ethnicity and culture. This is a prevalent and critical area of concern in our schools and we have devoted the next chapter to it.

Learning outcomes review

By reading this chapter, you will have been able to think about:

- The importance of developing empathy with characters in fiction and their situations
- Ways of exploring other lives
- The inclusion agenda and how differences can be both understood and celebrated
- Gender and children's literature

Questions for discussion

- How can we be sensitive to differences in the children we teach and their families when discussing children's literature?
- How would you respond to a parent or carer who complained about a focus on issues raised through children's literature and their subsequent discussion?

For your bookshelf

Blume, J. (1974) *Blubber*. London: Pan Macmillan.

This book deals sensitively with issues of bullying between schoolmates – in particular, how the bully can suddenly change her target so that a friend becomes the victim. Judy Blume's perception and humour make points well without ever labouring them.

Calder-Marshall, A. (1959) *The Fair to Middling*. London: Puffin.

This strange story has been out of print for some time, but is still available from online booksellers. The children in a school for 'Incapacitated Orphans' visit a strange fairground where they find the chance to become like everyone else, or accept themselves as they are. However, they come to realise that if they lose the disability that distinguishes them, what they will go on to achieve in life will also be changed and diminished. A good read with older classes in KS2.

Cook, J. (2019) *Uniquely Wired*. Boys Town, NE: Boys Town Press.

Zak is obsessed with watches. Before that it was trains. Zak also has autism, so he sometimes responds to the world around him in unconventional ways. This book deals clearly with many aspects of autism, explaining how the difference in perception of the world can cause problems. The colourful picture book format would make this a good book to share with a KS1 class who may find it hard to understand how a child with autism reacts so differently from others.

Bibliography

Baker, J. (1991) *Window*. London: Walker Books.
Bell, C. (2014) *El Deafo*. New York: Amulet Books.
Best, C. (2015) *My Three Best Friends and Me, Zulay*. New York: Margaret Ferguson Books.
Blume, J. (1973) *Deenie*. London: Macmillan.
Bösche, S. (1983) *Jenny Lives with Eric and Martin*. London: Gay Men's Press.
Cottle, K. (2020) *The Blue Giant*. London: Pavilion.
Fine, A. (1989) *Bill's New Frock*. London: Methuen.
Hall, M. (2015) *Red: A Crayon's Story*. London: HarperCollins.
Hart, C. (2019) *Together We Can*. London: Scholastic.
Laird, E. (2018) *Song of the Dolphin Boy*. London: Macmillan Children's Books.
Lawrence, C. (2006) *The Charioteer of Delphi*. London: Orion.

Lennon, J. (2017) *Touch the Earth.* New York: Simon & Schuster.
Platt, C. (2020) *The Story of Helen Keller: A Biography Book for New Readers.* Emeryville, CA: Rockridge Press.
Richardson, J. and Parnell, P. (2005) *And Tango Makes Three.* New York: Simon & Schuster.
Seuss, Dr. (1971) *The Lorax.* London: Random House.
Tharan Sanders, D. and Canzi, N. (2019) *Kaya's Heart Song.* London: Lantana Press.
Walliams, D. (2008) *The Boy in the Dress.* London: HarperCollins.
Wheatley, N. (1999) *Luke's Way of Looking.* London: Walker Books.

Further reading

Glazzard, J. and Stones, S. (2020) *Relationships Education for Primary Schools: A Practical Toolkit for Teachers.* St. Albins: Critical Publishing.

This book supports teachers to deliver the content of the DfE statutory guidance for relationships education in primary schools, introduced in 2020. It includes case studies and practical advice for teaching the topics of the new framework. Inclusion and pupil well-being are emphasised, as is the importance of partnerships with parents.

References

Bishop, R.S. (1990) Mirrors, windows, and sliding glass doors, *Perspectives: Choosing and Using Books for the Classroom,* 6 (3). Available at: https://scenicregional.org/wp-content/uploads/2017/08/Mirrors-Windows-and-Sliding-Glass-Doors.pdf (accessed 16 February 2022).
Braid, C. and Finch, B. (2015) 'Ah, I know why ...': Children developing understandings through engaging with a picture book, *Literacy,* 49 (3): 115–122.
Department for Education (DfE) (2011) *Teachers' Standards: Guidance for school leaders, school staff and governing bodies* updated 2013 and 2021). London: DfE. Available at: https://www.gov.uk/government/publications/teachers-standards.
Department for Education (DfE) (2013) *The National Curriculum in England: Key Stages 1 and 2 framework document.* London: DfE. Available at: https://www.gov.uk/government/publications/national-curriculum-in-england-primary-curriculum (accessed 30 July 2021).
Department for Education (DfE) (2019) *Relationships Education, Relationships and Sex Education (RSE) and Health Education: Statutory guidance for governing bodies, proprietors, head teachers, principals, senior leadership teams, teachers.* London: DfE. Available at: https://www.gov.uk/government/publications/relationships-education-relationships-and-sex-education-rse-and-health-education.
Kispal, A. (2008) *Effective Teaching of Inference Skills for Reading Literature Review.* London: DCSF. Available at: https://www.nfer.ac.uk/publications/edr01/edr01.pdf.
Narvaez, D. (2002) Individual differences that influence reading comprehension, in C.C. Block and M. Pressley (eds.) *Comprehension Instruction: Research Based Best Practices.* New York: Guilford Press.
Robinson, K. and Jones Diaz, C. (2005) *Diversity and Difference in Childhood: Issues for Theory and Practice.* Maidenhead: Open University Press.

5 Children's literature and different cultures

Learning outcomes

By reading this chapter, you will:

- Consider ways of making children's literature accessible to all
- Consider different examples of children's literature which explore different lives and experiences
- Explore literature as a stimulus for discussion and debate

Link to the Teachers' Standards

1. Set high expectations which inspire, motivate and challenge pupils

- establish a safe and stimulating environment for pupils, rooted in mutual respect
- set goals that stretch and challenge pupils of all backgrounds, abilities and dispositions
- demonstrate consistently the positive attitudes, values and behaviour which are expected of pupils

5. Adapt teaching to respond to the strengths and needs of all pupils

- have a secure understanding of how a range of factors can inhibit pupils' ability to learn, and how best to overcome these
- demonstrate an awareness of the physical, social and intellectual development of children, and know how to adapt teaching to support pupils' education at different stages of development
- have a clear understanding of the needs of all pupils, including those with special educational needs; those of high ability; those with English as an additional language; those with disabilities; and be able to use and evaluate distinctive teaching approaches to engage and support them

(DfE, 2011: 10–12)

Link to the National Curriculum

4.2 Teachers should take account of their duties under equal opportunities legislation that covers race, disability, sex, religion or belief, sexual orientation, pregnancy and maternity, and gender reassignment

4.6 The ability of pupils for whom English is an additional language to take part in the national curriculum may be in advance of their communication skills in English. Teachers should plan teaching opportunities to help pupils develop their English and should aim to provide the support pupils need to take part in all subjects.

(DfE, 2013: 8)

Our society and our schools become more richly diverse every year. Statistics for 2019, the most recent official figures at time of press, tell us that 33.5 per cent of pupils of primary school age are of minority ethnic origins, with pupils of Asian origin being the largest minority in all school types except pupil referral units (DfE, 2019: 7). In primary schools, the proportion of children whose English is a second or other language – those who speak another language in their home environment – is 21.2 per cent (2019: 8). Of course, there are huge regional and local variations – in some inner-city areas, the figure will be much higher, while there are small rural schools where a child whose origins are not local is a real rarity, but the national figures speak for themselves.

Activity

Perhaps you have experience in your own life which helps you appreciate the situation of the child growing up in a different culture? Or you have had holiday experiences where you didn't understand the speech of those around you? If so, you will realise the importance of inclusivity in this area. (If not, try tuning in to a television channel in another language – Welsh, perhaps, if you're not a Welsh-speaker! – for five minutes and see how it makes you feel.)

Think of books you have read, either as a child or later, where you identified with the main character. This is perhaps more likely to have been in childhood, where you can 'be' someone else in your head for hours at a time. Were they always of the same ethnicity as yourself? Did you feel apartness when reading about characters or families who were very different from your own, and did you find it harder to get completely into those stories?

There is growing concern that this diversity in society is not represented on our bookshelves. Indeed, the in their Reading Framework document, the Department for Education commented that 'Children also need to learn about the lives of those whose experiences and perspectives differ from their own' and maintained that choosing 'stories and non-fiction that explore such differences begins to break down a sense of otherness that often leads to division and prejudice' (DfE, 2021: 28). However, as the research focus below illustrates, it is challenging to find a range of appropriate texts when the majority of published works do not feature minority ethnic characters..

Research focus: The representation of different ethnicities in children's literature

Research by the Centre for Literacy in Primary Education (CLPE) found that only 10 per cent of the 6,478 children's books published in the UK in 2019 featured Black, Asian and other ethnic minority characters (Arts Professional, 2020: 1). The CLPE also found that in only 5 per cent of these books was a BAME character the main protagonist in the story (CLPE, 2020: 6). Although 'Asian heritage' is the largest identified group, with 6.8 per cent of children identifying this way, only 0.3 per cent of the books had an Asian-heritage main character, as opposed to, for instance, 2 per cent of the books featuring a Black African American or African Caribbean protagonist, although this group is only half as numerous at 3.4 per cent.

However, CLPE's 2021 report, which looked at the 5,875 children's picture books, fiction and non-fiction titles published in the UK in 2020, found that '879 featured characters of colour. Fifteen per cent of the children's picturebooks, fiction and non-fiction titles published in 2020 featured characters of colour, compared to 10 per cent in 2019, 7 per cent in 2018 and 4 per cent in 2017' (CLPE, 2021: 6).

CLPE concluded that: 'The continued positive trend in inclusive and representative output makes this a really exciting time in children's literature' (CLPE, 2021: 6). Clearly, this is better, but still not satisfactory. We need to represent all our children. There are many different ways of portraying different ethnicity in books. For instance, there are books for early readers whose illustrations show the characters as Black without any comment on this in the text. Well-known examples are *Peter's Chair* by Ezra Keats and *Corduroy* by Don Freeman, both of which recount universal experiences (reacting to a new sibling, and choosing a new toy) which can be shared by all children. Similarly, Ann Cameron's *The Julian Stories* and its successors tell simple stories of family life – the family in question is Black African American, though race is never referred to explicitly in the text and white readers can identify just as closely with, for example, winding up a younger brother, or accidentally eating all the dessert before the main meal. The classic *Amazing Grace*, by Mary Hoffman, has its protagonist being told by other children that she can't play Peter Pan because she is a girl, and because she's Black. This does not deter her, and after her grandmother has taken her to see a Black ballerina perform, Grace goes on to win the part and triumph in its performance. Here the race issue is raised and overcome, with an overarching positive message that anyone can achieve anything. The vivid and joyful pictures by Caroline Binch convey the atmosphere of Grace's family and home; her grandmother tells her traditional Anansi stories along with Western tales, but the world presented is a familiar one to most children.

The introduction of race and colour issues with young children is always going to be sensitive, and it would be easy to create tensions by discussion instead of alleviating them. The following case study shows how one teacher approached the issue.

Case study: Acceptance and diversity

Mehdi was aware that children in his Year 2 class had a wide range of ethnic backgrounds, and often stuck together in groups from similar families. He wanted to introduce the idea of diversity and inclusion, without specifically talking about colour, and decided to use Sarah Asuquo's book *Shine* as a starting point.

In the book, Kai is excited about starting back at school after the holidays, but finds he is on the end of hurtful remarks for being different. The pictures in the book show that Kai and his family are Afro-Caribbean, but the text does not refer to this. When Kai comes out of school sad, and his mother asks him what's wrong, Mehdi said before turning the page, 'I wonder why he's upset?' He had found before that this approach elicited more responses from the children than asking, 'Why is he upset?', because that suggested that there was one right answer which he knew.

Children suggested a range of answers about things which might have gone wrong at school, ranging from, 'He got into trouble' to 'He lost something'. Only two children suggested that he had been called names, and the examples they gave were racially slanted names.

It turns out in the story, though, that he has been called too tall. The next day there is a similar incident in which he is upset because someone has said his feet are too big! Eventually his parents reassure him that everyone is different and just as the moon and stars shine together but differently, so everyone can shine in their own special way. Kai passes the confidence this gives him on to another child, and the ending is happy and upbeat.

After reading the book with the class, Mehdi asked the children if they had been teased for being different. Everyone had some experience to share, from the boy with ginger hair and the girl with glasses, to the girl who was shouted at in the street when walking with her niqab-wearing sister. One girl said she thought it was 'silly to say people are different because of course they are'. Mehdi asked who agreed with this, and all hands went up. He asked how they could remember this, and the children wanted to make a sign saying 'Shine' and put it on their wall. They made this as a class project, and wrote a sentence each explaining the meaning, to be displayed around their sign.

Mehdi felt that he had successfully underlined the importance of acceptance and diversity without overtly raising issues of race or colour.

There is a growing canon of works in which there are characters from ethnic minority backgrounds, and in many of these race is not a specific issue. In David Walliams' *The Boy in the Dress*, for instance, the protagonist's best friend Darvesh is a Sikh. He has a very aspirational mother, which might seem to smack of stereotyping, and he wears a patka, about which the boys have one brief conversation, but apart from this his religion is completely immaterial to the story. It is perhaps interesting to note that in the Harry Potter canon, Cho Chang is first named in the third book, and Parvati and Padma Patil in the fourth. Their names are the only clue to their ethnic backgrounds. There are four other minor characters described as 'black' in the Potter series, but without any further comment.

A relatively early book to take on the topic of racism directly was Judy Blume's *Iggie's House*. Winnie's best friend has moved away to Japan, and the new family in her house, the Garbers, are Black Afro-Americans – the first in the neighbourhood. They meet with hostility from some – one neighbour in particular – and intend to move away again, then ultimately decide to stay. The story centres on Winnie, her attitude to the reactions she sees around her and her eagerness to befriend the new kids. Although some aspects of the situation are dated now, the book's ideas are still strong and make it a good read for older primary children.

It is increasingly important that all our children should grow up conscious of the issues that attitudes to race can raise in society. The case study below shows how one teacher started to do this in her school.

Case study: Raising awareness of prejudice

Sara, a Year 5 teacher in a city suburb school with a mixed-race catchment, wanted to raise her class's awareness of the prejudices that racism can express. Some of the children had seen footballers 'taking the knee' on television, and a Black Lives Matter graffito had been prominent on a bridge near the school and they wanted to know what it meant.

Without explaining what the object of the session would be, Sara started her session by dividing the class into two groups: all those with blue eyes were in one group, and the rest formed the other. She told this group they could sit down, but the blue-eyed group had to remain standing. She gave the blue-eyed group various jobs to do around the classroom and told them they were not allowed to speak, ask questions or say it wasn't fair. They also had to go regularly to their seated peers and ask them whether they could do anything for them – some asked for water bottles to be brought, or pencil cases fetched from the side, and one boy asked another to tie his shoelaces. This continued for five to ten minutes, and Sara then asked whether the class felt this had been fair. Unsurprisingly, both groups said it had not; they agreed it was stupid to treat people differently just because of the way they looked.

To follow this, Sara told the class that of course all lives matter, but explained that this had not always been seen as true. She told the children that until the middle of the twentieth century, many people in Britain and America had considered those with darker skin as inferior, and had not wanted or in many cases even allowed them to enjoy the same rights and privileges as white people. One or two of the children were aware of this, but it seemed strange to the majority. She introduced the word 'prejudice' and explained it to the class.

She then introduced the book *Iggie's House*, and told the class that although it had been written fifty years ago, it would help them understand some of the prejudices which Black families had faced in the USA. She chose to use extracts of two or three pages each rather than reading the whole book, to give the flavour; the book was available on the class library shelf, and she knew some children would follow it up. After explaining the basic set-up, she read them a section where a neighbour, Mrs. Landon, has called on Winnie's parents bringing a petition she wants them to sign ('I'm afraid it's rather unpleasant'), and expresses such ideas as 'Someone has to do something ... I just want our lovely neighbourhood to stay the way it is ... Let them know they won't be happy here. People rarely stay where they're not wanted' (Blume, 1970: 40–41). When Winnie asks her mother why she didn't sign the petition, the reply is, 'Because it really isn't any of our business, Winnie. Your father and I don't believe in getting mixed up in other people's lives. These things will work themselves out. Daddy and I are not crusaders' (1970: 68). When her ideas are not supported, this same woman puts a sign on the Garber family's lawn telling them they are not wanted in this area. This angers the family and they plan to move away. Sara then read a section from later in the story, in which Winnie has raised a petition of her own, asking neighbours to state their 'feelings about coloured people' [*sic*]. Her swimming teacher responds with, 'What colour? Green or purple?' and explains, 'I have many feelings. And my feelings are different for each person' (1970: 77). Eventually, Winnie comes to realise that the Garber family are just ordinary people, neither better nor worse than other families.

There was considerable reaction among the children when they heard the sections about the petition and the sign. Sara pointed out to the class that such things were now against the law, and considered race crimes. She explained the term racism. All agreed that the neighbour, Mrs. Landon, was racist, but there was some discussion as to whether Winnie's parents were racist by not wanting to get involved. Some children felt that Winnie could have done more to take an active anti-racist stand, and some felt that the Garber children themselves could have been more pro-active. They discussed whether such attitudes still existed, and many of the class were aware of such issues as footballers receiving racist abuse on social media, and press stories concerning royalty.

Sara hoped that the class would have understood from the story that in some racist situations it is not enough to say nothing, and that they would be better prepared to take an active stand.

The CLPE report also contains a useful list of questions to consider when looking at books depicting lives from ethnic minority groups (CLPE, 2020: 13–19), suggesting that such questions as social injustice and misconceptions, inclusion of characters who are not defined by their ethnicity, and helping to understand points of similarity and difference are all important in selecting texts for the classroom.

The website, Love Reading 4 Kids, has posted a wonderfully comprehensive list of *Diverse Voices – 80 Children's Books that Celebrate Difference* (2021), which contains titles for all age groups dealing with ethnically diverse situations. It includes both stories of conflict, in which diversity is an issue to be resolved, and stories simply set in another country or culture showing the familiarities of everyday life in contexts unfamiliar to some readers in modern Britain. There are also good biographies of characters such as Rosa Parks, Malala Yousafzai and Nelson Mandela, written for young readers. Such stories can play an important role in raising self-esteem, as well as understanding historical context.

Many children of non-British heritage in our schools are second- and third-generation British themselves. However, we also have a growing number of children arriving who may have found themselves in a situation they don't understand, at relatively short notice and without having chosen to be here. Such terms as 'migrants', 'immigrants', 'asylum seekers' and 'refugees' are so often heard on the news and in the press, often with negative connotations, that it is important for them to be understood.

The case study below explains how one teacher worked to raise awareness of these issues in his class.

Case study: Migration in children's literature

Jan had come to England as a small boy, with his family, and grown up in a city. He was distressed by seeing press headlines criticising immigrants and wanted to ensure that his Year 4 class would not adopt these attitudes.

He opened the session by writing on the board the words, Migrant / Refugee / Asylum seeker. He asked the class what they understood by these terms. Most of the children knew that the words referred to people who had moved to different countries, and some knew that refugees were those who could not return home, either because their homes had been destroyed or because they were in danger. Fewer were familiar with the term 'asylum seekers'. Jan explained that migrants are people who move around, either within their own country or to another, often, though not always, out of choice. He told them that his own father had migrated from Poland to find work in England, and this made him an immigrant, because immigrant just means someone who has travelled into another country. This surprised some of the children, and one girl commented that she 'thought immigrants were Black'.

He then explained that refugees cannot return to their own country or home, often because of wars or politics, and that many refugees then sought asylum – a safe place – in the country they had come to. If the government of the new country accepted them, they could then become legal citizens of their new home.

The class had recently been learning about World War II in History, so Jan decided that Judith Kerr's autobiographical *When Hitler Stole Pink Rabbit* would be a good text to use, because it would touch on a period and context they knew a little about, and would avoid discussion of complex current political situations. He also thought that Anna, the narrator, being the same age as his class at the beginning of the story would help them identify with the character.

He told the class that before the war, many German families had had to leave their homes and become refugees because they knew that otherwise they would be imprisoned.

Anna and her family had left their home in Berlin because her father, a writer, knew that the Nazis wanted to arrest him. They lived first in Switzerland, then Paris, and finally came to London. Jan read the children two long extracts – first, Anna's experience of attending school in Paris when she spoke only a few words of French, which included a section describing her feelings in the lesson she has just joined:

> 'As she listened she detected some numbers among the droning. Was it a multiplication table? She glanced at the book ... There was a picture of a king. Then it came to her. It was history! The numbers were dates and it had been a history lesson!'
>
> (Kerr, 1971: 172)

The extract (pp. 171–176) engaged the children's interest, and many had had similar experiences of such things as joining in a game they didn't understand, and getting the feeling that someone was friendly from a reassuring word ('Colette made a face at [the door] and said 'Ouf!' – p. 171).

Jan then read the section which describes the journey through the dark from Newhaven to London in a strange train (Kerr, 1971: 266–271). The children do not know where they are going, what to expect, or where they will sleep that night, and don't understand any of the conversation around them or the signs they see (from illuminated advertisements at stations, they decide that several English towns are called Bovril). Jan told the children that he could just remember that feeling from his own childhood journey, and asked if any of them had had a similar experience. Few of them had ever made a journey without their parents or family, but someone commented that the experience of a 'journey into the unknown' reminded them of the evacuees they had read about in Nina Bawden's *Carrie's War* and Shirley Hughes's *The Lion and the Unicorn*, which they had read in class. Jan asked the children to imagine how they would feel if they had no possessions except what was in their one bag, no understanding of the language around them, and the knowledge that they would never be going home again.

The creative writing produced after this session showed that the children had understood the concept of being a refugee, and would, Jan hoped, approach the subject with more empathy than they might have if they relied on newspaper headlines for their opinions.

There is an excellent article by Mairi Kidd of Amnesty International on 'Using text to explore asylum and migration in the classroom' (2018: 2–4), which gives a detailed study of how Frank Cottrell Boyce's *The Unforgotten Coat*, a story of two Mongolian brothers, can be used in the classroom to explore refugee experience. This article also contains a very useful list of books on many aspects of the topic, and is well worth seeking out. If you want to take the whole area of asylum seekers further, Amnesty International publish a clearly set-out and illustrated book of the Universal Declaration of Human Rights, called *We Are All Born Free* (2008), which could provide the stimulus for much classroom activity and discussion.

Research focus: Extremist views in children

A recent study by the Institute of Education, University of London, reported in *The Guardian* (Hall, 2021), found that extremist views and conspiracy theories among schoolchildren have risen considerably in the wake of such events as the risings in Afghanistan and the arrival of many new refugees from the Middle East. The study found that far right, misogynistic and Islamophobic views were increasingly heard in classrooms, and almost 90 per cent of teachers had heard conspiracy theories discussed. A trustee of Since 9/11, the body which commissioned the research, is quoted as saying: 'We must make sure that every pupil is taught how to reject extremist beliefs and ideologies ... we must use the power of education to fight back and help young people stand up to and reject extremism and violence.'

Another important consideration is, of course, language. Data released in 2013 from the 2011 census show that Polish has become the second most used language in the UK, with 546,000 people (1 per cent of the total population) using it as their main language. There are just over a million speakers of Indian subcontinental languages, divided between Panjabi, Bengali, Urdu and Gujarati (Office for National Statistics, 2013). Clearly we must be aware of this in our classrooms and acknowledge both the heritage of the non-native English speakers and the importance of helping them to progress in English.

If children have books at home, especially illustrated or picture books, which are in their own first language, encourage them to bring these into school and share them in a presentation to the rest of the class. Bi-lingual and multi-lingual texts are rarely found in the UK, but a child sharing a favourite story with her classmates can not only gain confidence in feeling her own heritage is validated, but also work on her own language skills as classmates supply the English words. This is a good exercise for the rest of the class too, as they work out the meanings of the unfamiliar sounds, and hear the rhythm and cadence of a different language. There is also an online resource, *World Stories*, run by the charity KidsOut, which offers free dual-text versions of more than 150 stories, often traditional folk tales, from the 21 most commonly spoken languages in the UK: children can listen, read in either or both languages, and watch the illustrations. This can be used for individual work, with small groups or a whole class, and can prove a valuable addition to a multi-lingual classroom. Children can both enjoy and celebrate their own culture and learn to become more at home in another. You will find other teaching resources and ideas for using the materials on this site as well.

Another good tool for inclusion is the graphic novel – either wordless, or with text. In the next chapter, you will find details of two books which can be especially useful in this context: Shaun Tan's *The Arrival*, which is wordless, and Victoria Jamieson and Omar Mohamed's *When Stars are Scattered.*

It is a daunting and bewildering experience to be alone in a roomful of strangers – perhaps you remember it from your first day at secondary school, or some other occasion? And it is so much more intense if you feel different, and you don't understand what people are saying, even if they seem friendly, and everything in your life is strange. As teachers, we need to make sure that we do whatever we can to help overcome these feelings. We hope that this chapter has given you some useful ideas on how we can help.

Learning outcomes review

By reading this chapter, you have:

- Considered ways of making children's literature accessible to all
- Considered different examples of children's literature which explore different lives and experiences
- Explored literature as a stimulus for discussion and debate

Questions for discussion

- What steps have you taken to ensure that the children's literature you offer represents the diverse nature of society?
- How confident do you feel about discussing issues which arise in children's literature?
- Is it ever appropriate to discuss race stereotypes in the classroom?
- Which is it more important to discuss – the differences in societies or the similarities?

For your bookshelf

Abdel-Magied, L. (2019) *You Must Be Layla*. London: Puffin.
A school story for KS2 which takes a familiar format – Layla starts at a new school, and gets into trouble for standing up to a bully – but Sudanese Layla's problems are caused by her hijab. Cheerful insights into Muslim family life, as well as giving a strong message about standing up for yourself.

Alston, B. (2021) *Amari and the Night Brothers*. London: Farshore.
A fantasy adventure for KS2 readers – the central character is a Black girl from a poor background, struggling to fit in as a scholarship girl at a private school, who finds a whole other world around her. First of a trilogy.

Meddour, W. (2020) *Lubna and Pebble*. Oxford: Oxford University Press.
A pebble is Lubna's only friend in the tent city where she and her family are living, until a lost boy arrives: an engaging story for younger children about the importance of kindness.

Mohammed, I. and Ali, S. (2019) *The Proudest Blue*. London: Andersen Press.
A book for younger children which discusses in a humorous and engaging way the importance and pride of wearing a hijab.

Morgan, M. (2012) *Walter Tull's Scrapbook*. London: Frances Lincoln Books.
The true story of Walter Tull, the Black orphan who was a star of Tottenham Hotspur and an officer in the Great War. Tull was nominated for a Military Cross, which was never awarded because of his colour, before he was killed on the Somme. The book is presented as an autobiographical scrapbook, and is fascinating and inspirational.

Singh Gangotra, M. (2021) *Sunflower Sisters*. Warwick: Owlet Press.
Two best friends, one of Indian and one of African heritage, are both looking forward to a big family wedding; the story explains different customs and families.

Waugh, D. (2015) *'Girls Can't Play Football!'*. Bishop's Castle: Constance Books.
Lauren's battle to play football despite resistance from some boys is the central theme of this story. Her ethnicity is irrelevant and never mentioned, and only revealed in an illustration on the final page.

Bibliography

Asuquo, S. (2020) *Shine*. Leicester: Troubadour Publishing.
Bawden, N. (1973) *Carrie's War*. London: Puffin.
Blume, J. (1970) *Iggie's House*. London: Bradbury Press.
Cameron, A. (1981) *The Julian Stories*. London: Random House.
Cottrell Boyce, F. (2011) *The Unforgotten Coat*. London: Walker Books.
Freeman, D. (1968) *Corduroy*. London: Viking.
Hoffman, M. (1991) *Amazing Grace*. London: Frances Lincoln Books.
Hughes, S. (1998) *The Lion and the Unicorn*. London: Red Fox.
Jamieson, V. and Mohamed, O. (2020) *When Stars are Scattered*. London: Random House.
Keats, E.J. (1967) *Peter's Chair*. London: Viking.

Kerr, J. (1971) *When Hitler Stole Pink Rabbit.* London: HarperCollins.
Tan, S. (2006) *The Arrival.* London: Hodder Children's Books.
Walliams, D. (2008) *The Boy in the Dress.* London: HarperCollins.

References

Amnesty International (2008) *We Are All Born Free.* London: Frances Lincoln Books.

Arts Professional (2020) *Ethnic representation in children's literature reaches new, low high.* Available at: https://www.artsprofessional.co.uk/news/ethnic-representation-childrens-literature-reaches-new-low-high (accessed 25 August 2021).

Centre for Literacy in Primary Education (CLPE) (2020) *Reflecting Realities.* Available at: https://clpe.org.uk/system/files/CLPE%20Reflecting%20Realities%202020.pdf (accessed 18 August 2021)

Centre for Literacy in Primary Education (CLPE) (2021) *Reflecting Realities: Survey of ethnic representation within UK children's literature 2020.* Available at: https://clpe.org.uk/system/files/2021-11/CLPE%20Reflecting%20Realities%20Report%202021.pdf (accessed 5 November 2021).

Department for Education (DfE) (2011) *Teachers' Standards: Guidance for school leaders, school staff and governing bodies* (updated 2013 and 2021). London: DfE. Available at: https://www.gov.uk/government/publications/teachers-standards (accessed 17 February 2022).

Department for Education (DfE) (2013) *The National Curriculum in England: Key Stages 1 and 2 framework document.* London: DfE. Available at: https://www.gov.uk/government/publications/national-curriculum-in-england-primary-curriculum (accessed 30 July 2021).

Department for Education (DfE) (2019) *Schools, Pupils and their Characteristics.* Available at: https://assets.publishing.service.gov.uk/government/uploads/system/uploads/attachment_data/file/812539/Schools_Pupils_and_their_Characteristics_2019_Main_Text.pdf (accessed 15 September 2021).

Department for Education (DfE) (2021) *The Reading Framework: Teaching the foundations of literacy.* London: DfE. Available at: https://assets.publishing.service.gov.uk/government/uploads/system/uploads/attachment_data/file/1000986/Reading_framework_Teaching_the_foundations_of_literacy_-_July-2021.pdf (accessed 15 August 2021).

Hall, R. (2021) Extreme views and conspiracy theories 'rising among pupils', *The Guardian*, 7 September. Available at: https://www.theguardian.com/education/2021/sep/07/extreme-views-and-conspiracism-rising-among-englands-pupils-research-finds (accessed 17 February 2022).

Kidd, M. (2018) Using text to explore asylum and migration in the classroom, *English 4–11*, 63: 2–4. Leicester: The English Association/UK Literary Association.

Love Reading 4 Kids (2021) *Diverse Voices – 80 Children's Books that Celebrate Difference.* Available at: https://www.lovereading4kids.co.uk/blog/collections/diverse-voices-childrens-books-that-celebrate-difference-6090 (accessed 22 September 2021).

Office for National Statistics (ONS) (2013) *Language in England and Wales.* London: ONS. Available at: https://www.ons.gov.uk/peoplepopulationandcommunity/culturalidentity/language/articles/languageinenglandandwales/2013-03-04 (accessed 25 August 2021).

World Stories. Leighton Buzzard: KidsOut. Available at: at https://www.kidsout.org.uk/what-we-do/world-stories/ (accessed 12 November 2021).

6 Engaging reluctant readers

Learning outcomes

By reading this chapter, you will consider:

- The importance of making reading a pleasurable activity for children
- How teachers can introduce children to texts which might appeal to reluctant readers
- The value of picture books, comics and graphic novels and some simple ways of engaging children's interest in them

Link to the Teachers' Standards

3. Demonstrate good subject and curriculum knowledge

- demonstrate an understanding of and take responsibility for promoting high standards of literacy, articulacy and the correct use of standard English

4. Plan and teach well structured lessons

- promote a love of learning and children's intellectual curiosity
- contribute to the design and provision of an engaging curriculum

(DfE, 2011: 11)

Link to the National Curriculum

Pupils should be taught to:

- develop pleasure in reading, motivation to read, vocabulary and understanding by:

- listening to and discussing a wide range of poems, stories and non-fiction at a level beyond that at which they can read independently
- being encouraged to link what they read or hear read to their own experiences
- becoming very familiar with key stories, fairy stories and traditional tales, retelling them and considering their particular characteristics
- recognising and joining in with predictable phrases
- learning to appreciate rhymes and poems, and to recite some by heart
- discussing word meanings, linking new meanings to those already known

(Year 1 Programme of Study, DfE, 2013: 21)

There have always been children who will state 'books are boring', say they 'don't like reading', and react with apathy to the sight of a book. In this chapter, we will show how you can address this in your classroom, and help you find texts, from picture books to graphic novels and e-books, which can give your reluctant readers a path to enjoying reading for pleasure.

Picture books are the usual starting point for readers, and children who have shared these from their early years have a head start in coming to love books. Picture books are usually defined as books with a lot of pictures and not much writing. This covers a huge range, from 'baby books' that have nothing but pictures (e.g. Helen Oxenbury's board books) or images with single-word captions, to linguistically sophisticated examples like the stories of Beatrix Potter.

In a picture book, beyond the very first ones, the story should be told both through a verbal and a visual narrative – so that a child who is not yet himself a reader but has shared the book with a reader, can turn the pages and tell himself the story even though most or all of the printed words may still be unrecognised. Writers of picture books often use devices such as rhymed text (e.g. Julia Donaldson's *The Gruffalo*), repetition of phrases (*Oh No, Anna!* by Vivian French) or sound effects (*We're Going on a Bear Hunt* by Michael Rosen) to encourage children to remember and predict the text, and come to recognise the printed forms of the words. Anyone who has ever tried to skip pages when reading a well-loved book to a toddler will know how well this works!

In good picture books, the pictures add detail to the simple text, so that the text can be extended by discussing the pictures. Look at the details – for instance, the school fete in *Dogger* by Shirley Hughes and the street in *The Tiger Who Came to Tea* by Judith Kerr.

Activity

Think of the first books which you remember from childhood.

- What's the first thing you recall – the pictures or the words?
- Are there images that stayed with you – pictures you imagined yourself inside, or maybe pages you tried not to look at because they were scary?
- Did you like pictures where you could recognise familiar things from your own life, or ones that created a whole different world for you?

If you are remembering and re-seeing these pictures in your mind now, after a long gap, you will realise how important the visual element of books is, especially to those who aren't yet able to decode the written words!

Many picture books are available on YouTube. A good exercise is to watch these with the sound off – if you can follow the story clearly, it works as a picture book! An excellent example for this is Shirley Hughes's *Alfie Gets in First*. The text doesn't appear on the screen, but the facial expressions and the detailed pictures make the story absolutely clear.

There are also books in which the pictures can tell a whole parallel story. John Burningham's *Time to Get Out of the Bath, Shirley* and *Come Away from the Water, Shirley* are excellent examples. On one page we see real life (bathtime, or playing on the beach) narrated by the remarks of parents, while on the facing page – wordless – are the wonderful adventures of the little girl's imagination.

Some picture books have overtones of a different dimension. Is the monster who eats Bernard in David McKee's *Not Now, Bernard* real? (And if so, why don't his parents notice?) Does Max in Maurice Sendak's *Where the Wild Things Are* really travel to a distant island? (And if so, why is his supper still hot when he gets back?) Are these actually representations of temper tantrums or some other crisis in a child's life, intended to reassure the reader of the permanence and comprehensiveness of parents' love – and does this aspect matter?

So, once the child's interest in books as interesting objects has been kindled by picture books, how do we go from there to encourage interest in the written word? A multi-media approach can be a huge help here. Many stories told on YouTube have the text displayed as you listen, in various formats. During the lockdown summer of 2020, when many parents and carers were responsible for home-schooling their children, one tip which was widely shared was always to have the sub-titles on while watching television with children, so that they are exposed to the written word and understand that it's an element of communication.

There are many comics on the market aimed at young children and pre-readers; almost all of these are tie-ins with popular television or film characters such as Disney princesses or Thomas the Tank Engine. Although they are not designed for classroom use, nearly all of them contain some activities involving recognising words or letters, and the text accompanying the picture stories can be read with children. Many words (beautiful, mischievous, ocean, exciting), which may be well beyond their reading level, will be seen as the children look at the pictures and subliminally their shapes can gradually become recognised.

And from comics, a growing number of children progress to comic books. This has led to a growing discussion about whether comic books count as 'real reading'; they are sometimes regarded as a modern phenomenon, although the genre has been going since at least the 1830s. An early Swiss writer of cartoon books, Rodolphe Topffer, said in 1837 of such work, 'He who uses such a direct method will have the advantage over those who talk in chapters' (Perry, 1971: 17). Although these works were disapproved of for a long time, there is an increasing swing to recognising the benefits which this genre can bring to readers who find it difficult to engage with a whole page of solid text. First of all, of course, they look interesting. Many are brightly coloured and action-packed, encouraging a child to give them attention. Children with dyslexia have clues in the pictures to help them recognise words; in many cases, emotions and feelings can be identified from pictures. Because there is no linking text or description, the reader's powers of inference can be developed as the sequencing of the story is followed. Comic books also give even confident readers a unique opportunity to acquire new vocabulary in combination with context cues, that is, information from pictures to help children decipher the meaning of unfamiliar words.

Research focus: Reading for pleasure

The government report on Reading for Pleasure stated that research has found 'a slight increase in the proportion of children who claim to be reading comics/comic books and newspapers at least once or twice a week in England' (DfE, 2012: 5), although 'reading comic books is associated with little improvement in reading proficiency in some countries, and with lower overall reading performance in other countries' (2012: 13). This perception is probably a legacy from various US studies in the 1950s, which suggested that 'comic books [were] a motivating factor in youthful disturbance ... too violent, too sexual, and too bloody' (Wertham, 1954: 16). However, the format has developed and extended its range considerably since then, and indeed has never had this image in some societies – France, for instance, where *bandes dessinées* are recognised as an official art form, and Japan where *manga* has been seen as an important element of cultural heritage since the 1870s.

A recent paper on a project to use comic-strip formats in the teaching of science concluded that 'reading comics is not a passive activity because, while reading comics, the reader should complete the gaps between the panels that requires active thinking' (Özdemir and Eryilmaz, 2019: 3), and found that Year 6 children were much more ready to engage with information presented and assessed in this way. The appeal of the format, whether as a teaching tool or a reading choice, is widely supported and can bring reluctant readers to the pleasure of the written word, albeit by a scenic route.

As Roald Dahl (1989) wrote in a recently auctioned letter, the content of any children's book is '... of no importance other than that it enthrals the child – and thus it teaches or seduces him or her to "like" books and to become a fit reader – which is vital if that child is going to amount to anything in later life.' Dahl concluded: 'The book-reading child will always outstrip the non-book-reading child in later life. There are very few messages in these books of mine. They are there simply to turn the child into a reader of books'.

As the research cited above suggests, although picture books are for most children the way in to reading, they are by no means limited to small children in their appeal. There is a growing proliferation of books with little text, or with as much illustrative content as verbal, whose target readership is way beyond early reader stage.

A good example of this is Maurice Sendak's *Outside Over There*, a beautifully illustrated book with only 359 words of text, listed on several websites as 'for 6–9-year-olds'. When first published, the book was placed on the publisher's adult reading catalogue; certainly any parent who bought it hoping for a successor to *Where the Wild Things Are* might be alarmed by the story of a stolen baby, an ice-baby who melts away, and disturbingly realistic goblin-babies who are forced to dance until they dissolve in sickness. It's a beautiful picture book, but not for small children.

There will always be children who choose to be challenged and want to read books beyond their prescribed age-level, just as they are keen to tackle extension tasks in other subjects. Similarly, there are children who prefer reassurance and will choose a book they know they will find easy, or revisit the known world of a familiar book. When we visit a library or bookshop, we are not told which shelves to browse from. While we may make suggestions about which books children could select, it is important that we always stay aware that it must be their choice. This book is concerned with the pleasure of reading; a book chosen because you want to read it is more likely to achieve this than a book a teacher has told you to read.

In Chapter 1, you read about how a 'reading partner' system can work to the advantage of different year-groups in a school. The case study below demonstrates another way in which looking at books together can overcome the perceived boundaries of age-appropriateness.

Case study: *The Arrival*

Jessica noticed that one boy in her class, Luke, usually chose books without words from the class reading shelves although his reading skills were at the appropriate level for his age, and that sometimes other children teased him about this. She decided to approach this by studying a wordless book together in class, and chose Shaun Tan's *The Arrival* as her material. Several children in her class had had the experience of coming to start a new life in England from different cultures, and she hoped this would help them too, to consider their own situation in context.

Jessica chose to use the video of the first section, so that all the class would be able to see the images clearly and she could pause it for discussion. First, she showed the opening section, which shows a man taking a photo of his family from the wall and wrapping it carefully. This led to discussion as to why he was doing this, where he might be going and why.

As the story unfolds, we see that his home city is beset by some giant tentacled creatures, and the man, like many others from his city, is seeking a new life in a different country a long sea voyage away. The story goes on to show how everything is strange and incomprehensible to him as he seeks a home and a job in his new world, and how the picture of his family remains an important talisman. Throughout the story, detailed and lifelike figures are mixed with fantastical buildings, strange creatures and incomprehensible inscriptions, which were a good stimulus for discussion. For instance, as the ship crowded with immigrants nears the harbour of its destination, there is an image showing the sky above them crowded with what look like origami birds made of white paper (at 3.05). Jessica asked the class if they thought these were real birds. About half of the children thought they were real; others suggested that they were decorations sent out to welcome the ship, like balloons, or had been made by the travellers during the voyage. One girl thought that perhaps they were not real and might be 'all the dreams of the people on the ship'. Jessica asked what dreams the travellers might have at this point, and the idea emerged that they would be full of hopes and ideas about their new lives. After collecting and sharing some ideas about this, Jessica asked the children each to choose one person shown in the image and write a paragraph telling this person's thoughts. Later she printed out this image and created a display with the children's writing added as 'thought bubbles' .

She then showed the story as far as the point where the man is settling into a room where familiar elements (a chair, a window) are mixed with strange and alien artefacts and creatures. Jessica invited the class to remember times when they had been in a strange situation with things they didn't understand. Some of the children with memories of arrival in the UK were able to describe early confusions and problems. One boy told of putting sweet wrappers carefully into the red bin on the street, until a neighbour informed him it was a post box. Several children talked of how bewildered they had felt on their first day at school. Not all of the children who had direct experience of arriving to live in a new country chose to contribute, but they showed involvement in the discussion.

At the end of this session, Jessica asked the class why they thought the author had chosen to tell his story without words. There was general agreement that it was better 'because everyone could put their own story into it'. One boy said, 'He shows you the story and you can tell it to yourself.'

The term 'comic books' has largely been superseded in education circles by 'graphic novels'. Is there a distinction? It seems to be generally agreed (Britannica, Oxford English Dictionary, dictionary.cambridge.org) in definitions that graphic novels are longer, and tell a single complete narrative, while comic books are those which, shorter in form, recount episodes in a continuing narrative with a recurring set of characters. When children read enjoyable, complex and compelling stories, they are motivated to read more, so graphic novels can be great stepping-stones to longer text works. Many well-loved and classic works have now been produced in graphic formats, including *The Witches* (Roald Dahl), *Anne of Green Gables* (Lucy Maud Montgomery), *A Wrinkle in Time* (Madeleine L'Engle), *Artemis Fowl* (Eoin Colfer) and the *Adventures of John Blake* series by Philip Pullman.

Graphic novels can show situations and emotions more immediately and engagingly than pages of careful description which some readers will skip or skim. For this reason, they are a good way to approach sensitive or complicated emotional areas and topics, and excellent new examples are emerging all the time. Jerry Craft's *New Kid*, telling the story of a 12-year-old boy's life in a school where there are very few non-white students like him, was the first graphic novel to win the USA's prestigious Newbery Prize, in 2020. *When Stars Are Scattered*, by Victoria Jamieson and Omar Mohamed, is the true story of a Somali boy in a Kenyan refugee camp and his struggle to attend school and to build a better life for himself and his little brother. The story addresses many complex issues, and was told by the boy Omar Mohamed to the author who has illustrated it. Such books as these can bring awareness of very different lives vividly into the classroom.

Activity

Choose a short passage – perhaps a couple of pages – from a favourite book. Then 'story-board' it in up to six pictures. You can use speech or thought bubbles, but with not more than a couple of sentences in each. Then compare the two versions.

- Have you managed to include visual details from the text?
- Have you added any details from your imagination?
- Did you find it easy to show, for instance, how characters were feeling?
- Do you think the story would be easier, as easy, or harder to follow from your picture version?
- Would you introduce this as a class activity? If so,
  - How would you respond to the child who says, 'I can't draw'?
  - Would you make it an individual or a group activity?
  - What do you think the children would gain or learn from doing this?

There is also a growing number of what may be termed 'halfway house' books, such as Liz Pichon's *Tom Gates* series and Jeff Kinney's *Wimpy Kid* books, where a text narrative is liberally illustrated throughout with cartoon-style drawings. These are particularly popular with boys, and can help seduce reluctant readers towards enjoying written text.

The other great and ever-growing area of literature to consider is, of course, the e-book. It is undeniable that each successive cohort of children coming into our classrooms is more and more familiar with using a computer or tablet, and many in Reception classes have already sophisticated technology skills by the time they start school. What could be more natural, then, than starting their reading journey with e-books, of which there is a vast range? Some advantages immediately come to mind:

- The reader is using a familiar reading environment and feels comfortable with it.
- E-books are more eco-friendly than what is sometimes called the DTP – the 'Dead Tree Press'. They need no paper to produce and, although of course the energy used by devices must be factored in, represent a better deal for the planet.
- They are considerably cheaper than paper books for a school to purchase – no small consideration.
- The book is in a durable form – no worries about sticky fingers or torn pages!
- Font size and sometimes colours can be easily changed, making text more accessible for those with any visual disability.
- Many e-books contain embedded audio and video enhancements, to keep younger readers engaged.

However, there are of course concerns about and disadvantages to the use of e-books. The effect on health of too much time spent online, and the eye-strain which can be the result of the glare from a screen are frequently cited as worries; power can fail; the constant awareness of other on-screen options can be distracting; embedded hypertext links to follow can prevent the reading being as totally immersive an experience as can be obtained from a traditional paper book. Also, there is the thought that an e-book is perhaps a more ephemeral experience, and will not give the pleasure of holding and re-reading an 'old favourite' book over years. This idea was perhaps best summed up by developmental psychologist and cognitive scientist Maryanne Wolf: 'There is physicality in reading, maybe even more than we want to think about as we lurch into digital reading – as we move forward perhaps with too little reflection. I would like to preserve the absolute best of older forms, but know when to use the new' (quoted in Picton, 2014: 13).

Research focus: e-books

A study by the Literacy Trust suggests that there are considerable benefits to the use of e-books. Trials were held in a number of schools with varying demographics and age groups involved. Participating schools designed their own projects with a focus group of pupils, who would work for this project using e-platforms instead of conventional printed materials. The results were interesting. The study found that over the course of the project, which lasted for an average of 4.2 months, boys' reading levels increased by an average of 8.4 months, compared to 7.2 months' progress made by girls. Furthermore, the percentage of boys that felt reading was difficult almost halved from 28.0 per cent to 15.9 per cent, suggesting that confidence in their own reading ability increased as a result of the project. In addition, the percentage that felt reading was cool rose from 34.4 per cent to 66.5 per cent (Picton and Clark, 2015: 23).

The National Literacy Trust's annual literacy survey questions thousands of children and young people aged 8 to 16 about their literacy behaviours. In 2012, children reported reading more on computers and other electronic devices than in print form for the first time, confirming the central role of technology in young people's literacy lives (Picton, 2014: 4). This survey also reported significant improvement in reading speed and comprehension skills of students with dyslexia when using texts on-screen rather than on paper (2014: 5).

There are always concerns about the use of screen activities in the classroom, whether it be the worry that children may be exposed to age-inappropriate content, damaging their eyes by having too much screen time, or using devices for other activities (see Dierking, 2015). There are regular calls from politicians and other bodies to ban the use of mobile phones and other devices from classrooms. However, there is evidence that schools and teachers are increasingly using teaching strategies which use technology wisely and judiciously and that 'technological equipment allows the personalization of learning paths and educational inclusion of a flexible organization' (Marzano et al., 2013: 4). In a world where 'digital literacy should be the fourth pillar of a child's education alongside reading, writing and mathematics, and be resourced and taught accordingly' (House of Lords Report, 2017: para. 317), it is better to embrace the change and use it to our advantage.

Reading in lockdown

The lockdown and home-schooling periods of 2020 and 2021 will have broadened many parents' and teachers' understanding and ideas of e-books and their uses. At the time of writing, there has not yet been any national survey relating to this period published, but anecdotal and informal evidence suggests that there is a wider acceptance of the use of technology. It's the future!

Case study: Online texts in lockdown

During the lockdown periods of 2020 and 2021, many children were confined to their home environment with no physical access to school, shops or libraries. Oak National Academy, a government-backed virtual school, launched a virtual library so that pupils could read books from popular children's authors digitally.

The library was formed with the National Literacy Trust, after measures were taken to close schools in England to the majority of pupils. Children were provided with a free-to-access book every week from the library's author of the week, in an initiative aiming to increase access to e-books and audiobooks for the most disadvantaged young readers during closures and support the literacy of children most affected by Covid-19. Jacqueline Wilson's *The Story of Tracy Beaker*, illustrated by Nick Sharratt, was the first book to feature and was free to access and read for a week in January 2021.

Maria, a Year 4 teacher, wanted to keep in touch with her class's reading during this time when she was unable to be with them. She knew that many would not have books in their homes, and chose to use this online resource as a class library. Each week she asked the class to read the library's choice of the week, and she prepared questions and activities for regular Friday Zoom sessions in which the books were discussed, She followed each session by assigning a short written task related to the book, which the children could send by e-mail. Not all the children joined every week, and some were limited in participation by poor connections or by having to use mobile phones, but the response was generally good and when Maria was able to meet the class again in person, several children said both that they had read and enjoyed books they wouldn't have chosen otherwise and that they had enjoyed being able to read a 'set book' as and when they chose rather than sitting in a classroom.

Maria felt that she had helped to keep the class's reading habits going during the lockdowns, and from remarks made by some of the children she felt that some who did not particularly enjoy 'doing' a book in class might continue their reading online with more enthusiasm.

This chapter has suggested several ways in which you can help to bring the reluctant reader to an enjoyment of books and reading. There is a book out there for everyone – it's just a question of finding the right one. And you are sure to make many interesting discoveries yourself as you help guide the search.

Learning outcomes review

By reading this chapter, you have considered:

- The importance of making reading a pleasurable activity for children

- How teachers can introduce children to texts which might appeal to reluctant readers
- The value of picture books, comics and graphic novels and some simple ways of engaging children's interest in them

Questions for discussion

- Can you think of examples of children or adults who became enthusiastic readers after previously being reluctant readers? What do you think changed their attitudes?
- Think of some of the children you work with who are reluctant readers. How might you try to turn them into enthusiastic readers?
- Do you think your school provides a sufficiently wide range of text types and means of reading to enable all children to engage with reading for pleasure?

For your bookshelf

Many of the books mentioned in Chapters 4 and 5 can also be good resources for reluctant readers. Here are three more suggestions which you may find useful.

Gaiman, N. (2003) *The Wolves in the Walls*. London: Bloomsbury.
An extraordinary story full of humour and suspense, about facing up to fears. The artwork combines drawings, photography and computer-generated images. It looks like a picture book but has appeal to older children. Its very difference can appeal to and engage children who aren't interested in the ordinary.

Rosen, M. (2011) *Sad Book*. London: Walker Books.
This picture book, with simple, short, text, tells of the writer's feelings after the death of his son. It's a valuable exploration into feelings not usually found in children's books, and could be invaluable for helping children who are coping with feelings of grief and loss which they have difficulty in expressing.

Tan, S. (2010) *The Lost Thing*. London: Hodder Children's Books.
Another picture book with minimal text, this is both humorous and a comment on alienation, strangeness and noticing what is around you. It's one of those books which can mean something different to each reader. There's an animated version on YouTube at https://www.youtube.com/watch?v=rpak6ktsux4.

Bibliography

Burningham, J. (1977) *Come Away from the Water, Shirley*. London: Jonathan Cape.
Burningham, J. (1978) *Time to Get Out of the Bath, Shirley*. London: Jonathan Cape.

Craft, J. (2019) *New Kid*. New York: Barnes & Noble.
Donaldson, J. (1999) *The Gruffalo*. London: Macmillan Children's Books.
French, V. (1997) *Oh No, Anna!*. London: Gullane Children's Books.
Hughes, S. (1977) *Dogger*. London: Bodley Head.
Hughes, S. (1981) *Alfie Gets in First*. London: Bodley Head.
Jamieson, V. and Mohamed, O. (2020) *When Stars are Scattered*. London: Random House.
Kerr, J. (1968) *The Tiger Who Came to Tea*. London: HarperCollins.
McKee, D. (1980) *Not Now, Bernard*. London: Andersen Press.
Rosen, M. (1989) *We're Going on a Bear Hunt*. London: Walker Books.
Sendak, M. (1963) *Where the Wild Things Are*. London: Harper & Row.
Sendak, M. (1981) *Outside Over There*. London: Harper & Row.
Tan, S. (2006) *The Arrival*. London: Hodder Children's Books.
Wilson, J. (1991) *The Story of Tracy Beaker*. London: Doubleday.

Further reading

Dierking, R. (2015) Using nooks to hook reluctant readers, *Adolescent and Adult Literacy*, 58 (5): 407–416.

Dierking conducted research in a US high school which adopted electronic reading devices with free-choice, silent, sustained reading for previously reluctant readers. The author describes both the benefits and challenges of using e-readers.

References

Dahl, R. (1989) Letter to Christine Wotton, dated 2 August. *itvNEWS*, 15 June 2021. Available at: https://www.itv.com/news/central/2021-05-20/handwritten-letter-by-roald-dahl-telling-his-secrets-to-storytelling-to-go-on-sale-at-staffordshire-auction (accessed 17 February 2022).

Department for Education (DfE) (2011) *Teachers' Standards: Guidance for school leaders, school staff and governing bodies* (updated 2013 and 2021). London: DfE. Available at: https://www.gov.uk/government/publications/teachers-standards (accessed 16 February 2022).

Department for Education (DfE) (2012) *Research Evidence on Reading for Pleasure*. London: DfE. Available at: https://assets.publishing.service.gov.uk/government/uploads/system/uploads/attachment_data/file/284286/reading_for_pleasure.pdf (accessed 27 May 2021).

Department for Education (DfE) (2013) *The National Curriculum in England: Key Stages 1 and 2 framework document*. London: DfE. Available at: https://www.gov.uk/government/publications/national-curriculum-in-england-primary-curriculum (accessed 30 July 2021).

Dierking, R. (2015) Using nooks to hook reluctant readers, *Adolescent and Adult Literacy*, 58 (5): 407–416.

House of Lords (2017) *Growing Up With the Internet: Summary of conclusions and recommendations*. Available at: https://publications.parliament.uk/pa/ld201617/ldselect/ldcomuni/130/13004.htm (accessed 17 February 2022).

Marzano, A., Tammaro, R., Notti, A.M., D'Alessio, A. and Stasio, D. (2013) The use of ebooks in education to improve learning, Proceedings of EDULEARN13 Conference,

1–3 July, Barcelona. Available at: https://www.academia.edu/11784025/THE_USE_OF_EBOOKS_IN_EDUCATION_TO_IMPROVE_LEARNING (accessed 1 July 2021).
Özdemir, E. and Eryilmaz, A. (2019) Comics in science teaching: A case of speech balloon completing activity for health related concepts, *Journal of Inquiry Based Activities*, 9 (1): 37–51. Available at: https://files.eric.ed.gov/fulltext/ED595642.pdf (accessed 26 May 2021).
Perry, G. (1971) *The Penguin Book of Comics*. London: Penguin.
Picton, I. (2014) *The Impact of eBooks on the Reading Motivation and Reading Skills of Children and Young People: A rapid literature review*. London: National Literacy Trust. Available at: https://eric.ed.gov/?id=ED560635.
Picton, I. and Clark, C. (2015) *The Impact of eBooks on the Reading Motivation and Reading Skills of Children and Young People: A study of schools using RM Books. Final Report*. London: National Literacy Trust. Available at: https://eric.ed.gov/?id=ED570688 (accessed 17 February 2022).
Wertham, F. (1954) *Seduction of the Innocent*. New York: Rinehart.

Classic literature

Learning outcomes

By reading this chapter, you will:

- Consider what is meant by classic children's literature
- Identify some texts regarded as classic children's literature
- Consider how we define a classic
- Think about why we read classic books with children
- Understand and critique the 'Golden Age' of children's books
- Reflect on the issue of modern classics
- Consider how we can introduce adult classics to children

Link to the Teachers' Standards

3. Demonstrate good subject and curriculum knowledge

- demonstrate an understanding of and take responsibility for promoting high standards of literacy, articulacy and the correct use of standard English

4. Plan and teach well structured lessons

- promote a love of learning and children's intellectual curiosity
- contribute to the design and provision of an engaging curriculum

(DfE, 2011: 11)

Link to the National Curriculum

Pupils should be taught to:

- develop pleasure in reading, motivation to read, vocabulary and understanding by:
  - listening to, discussing and expressing views about a wide range of contemporary and classic poetry, stories and non-fiction at a level beyond that at which they can read independently

(Year 2 Programme of Study, DfE, 2013: 28)

Classic literature! What do the words say to you? Does your mind instantly fill with images of Jim Hawkins, Alice, Kay Harker, Winnie the Pooh, Sara Crewe, the White Witch, the March girls and Tom Sawyer? Or is your first reaction, 'boring old-fashioned stuff'? If so, this chapter will try to convince you of the pleasure of sharing books which have been loved for generations, and the benefits of introducing the classics in your classroom.

Activity

Write a list of ten or twelve books you loved as a child. Now look at your list and decide which ones you would call classics.

- How did you decide?
- Of the 'classics' books, which did you first meet at school?
- How did you feel when you first read these books?
- Have you re-read them recently, and if so, did you still feel the same?
- If you can, compare your list with that of a friend. Do you have books in common?

There are many books which children are likely to pick up for themselves, in a bookshop or library, either because they have seen the television or film version, because the author is a celebrity they are familiar with, or because there is something eye-catching or exciting on the cover. And this is fine, because all reading, just about, is good reading. As a teacher, then, perhaps you can broaden horizons beyond the obvious and introduce your class to characters and worlds which will stay with them and sustain them for years. Most children go through at least one phase of feeling themselves alienated, isolated and different from those around them; it can be enormously reassuring to find someone in fiction who is undergoing the same experience.

Many of the books regarded today as children's classics were written between the 1860s and the 1920s. This is sometimes called the 'Golden Age' of children's literature, because it was the time in which the idea of writing stories specifically for children to enjoy first took off. Until then, reading for children was dominated by Locke's edict that fantasy and fairy stories were 'perfectly useless trumpery' (Locke, 1693/2020). Fare for children had been mostly books of nursery rhymes like those of Kate Greenaway, or passages from such books as *Robinson Crusoe* (Daniel Defoe, 1719) or *Gulliver's Travels* (Jonathan Swift, 1726). Although these books contained appealingly fanciful ideas, in part, and have both been made into children's films, they were vehicles for serious philosophical, political and theological ideas, and would have proved heavy going for any child who took on the whole work. Charles and Mary Lamb's *Tales from Shakespeare* appeared in 1807, designed to familiarise young people with the stories and plots of the plays while excising many of the complications of sub-plots and dramatic structure. This was an unusual effort, though; for the most part, children were expected to stick to nursery fare until they could cope with reading at an adult level. The increase in education and literacy, and the growth of the

Sunday School movement, gave rise to a great increase in demand for books suitable for children at the end of the nineteenth century, and publishers such as the Society for the Promotion of Christian Knowledge (founded in 1698) began to produce many volumes suitable for prize presentation. In these, good is always rewarded and naughtiness punished or atoned for by sacrifice, and a high moral tone prevails throughout. The popularity of these accounts, perhaps, for the prevalence of morality themes in many early children's books. Perhaps the apotheosis of these is Mrs. Sherwood's *History of the Fairchild Family* (1818), in which a moralising father takes his children to see corpses rotting on a gibbet to teach them about mortality. This was a classic best-seller in its day, inflicted on thousands of Victorian children!

As Carpenter (1985: 1) comments, 'Adults ... want to feed the children a set of moral examples. By all means let them have their fun, but the opportunity of feeding them a set of moral examples is not to be wasted.'

Several of the early books written for children were created specifically to make a social or political point. Anna Sewell's *Black Beauty* (1877), for instance, was to draw attention to the conditions of cab-horses in Victorian London. Charles Kingsley's *The Water-Babies* (1863) made readers aware of the situation of child chimney-sweeps, as well as being a vehicle for the author's commentaries on current educational and scientific theories. Rudyard Kipling's *Stalky and Co.* (1899) was arguably 'to demonstrate that boyish anti-authoritarian pranks at school are a good training for manly service in the cause of one's nation' (Carpenter, 1985: 15). The majority, however, stick more or less overtly to the message that good will always be rewarded. Alison Lurie has commented, 'The usual manner is that of a kind lady or gentleman delivering a delightfully disguised sermon' (1990: 118). It is not until the turn of the century and the arrival of such writers as E. Nesbit that the revolutionary idea that sometimes naughtiness turns out all right is introduced.

So, why would we want to read these books in the classroom when there are so many excellent modern books around, which deal with contemporary life and address issues unmentioned in most of these classics? One simple reason is because they are good stories, with strong and memorable characters. A good story can transport us into worlds or societies of which we have no experience in life, and make them real to us. When the imagination is engaged, the reader can feel the experience of flying through the night sky, having tea with a faun, or exploring unknown territories in a totally immersive way. As Aleksandr Solzhenitsyn said in his 1970 Nobel Lecture in Literature:

> The only substitute for an experience we ourselves have never lived through is art, literature. They possess a wonderful ability: beyond distinctions of language, custom, social structure, they can convey the life experience of one whole nation to another ... Literature conveys irrefutable condensed experience ... from generation to generation. Thus it becomes the living memory of the nation.

So, although the situation may be strange, a fictional character's feelings and reactions are 'human' – readers may never have had twelve dwarves turn up unexpectedly for tea, or been sent on a mission to find a dragon's gold, but Bilbo's irritation and alarm enable the reader to share the experience.

Activity

It has often been said that there are only seven types of story:

- Comedy – not necessarily 'a laugh a line', but light-hearted and with a happy ending
- Tragedy – inescapable doom, and everything ending badly. Not, thankfully, common in children's books these days
- Rags to riches – a fundamental change of circumstances, however brought about
- The Quest – setting out for an important goal which is, usually, beyond the personal
- Overcoming the Monster – defeating a physical or psychological problem, or an enemy
- Voyage and Return
- Rebirth – the protagonist has changed in one or more important ways by the end of the story

Of course, these very often overlap and you will find more than one theme in a book. Think of books you know – perhaps those you listed at the beginning of this chapter. Do you agree that all the events can fit into one or more of these descriptions? Do you think it's helpful to spot these themes? Or can you think of an eighth category?

Another good argument for classic literature in schools is that such books are generally written in a full, elegant and formal style. Reading a well-written book teaches children much about good writing practice by giving them sound models. Many of today's best-sellers feature lots of short sentences, exclamation marks, changes in typeface, and lengthy phonetic representations of exciting sound effects. These are fine occasionally, and encourage reluctant readers to persevere – but children should have access to a range of styles and vocabularies. In classic literature there are no hashtags, emojis or abbreviated codes, just clear narration and dialogue. A good author will enrich the reader's range without it even being noticed. For instance, in Beatrix Potter's *The Tale of Peter Rabbit*, a very early reader for most children, the sparrows 'implored [Peter] to exert himself'. Not necessarily the words you would choose for speaking to small children, but swallowed whole without question because they are met in the middle of a story, and the meaning is clear from the context.

The issue of accessibility was not one which would have been considered at the time when many classics were written, because the readers would have been a fairly narrow set of well-educated children for whom the complexity of vocabulary and structure would not have proved impenetrable. A more straightforward style is obviously desirable nowadays if a book is truly to be accessible for all; however, as the journalist Adrian Chiles (2021) wrote when discussing *The Wind in the Willows* (Kenneth Grahame, 1908), 'we marvel at the beauty and mystery of the language; a little bewilderment here and there is no bad thing'.

Many classic books have also become embedded in British culture and everyday conversation, and this might be another reason for children to encounter the originals. Just as adults might be expected to recognise well-known quotations from Shakespeare, or to know where 'I wandered, lonely as a cloud' comes from, so children meeting such phrases as 'grinning like a Cheshire cat', 'time for a little something', or 'do as you would be done by' will understand the allusion better if they have seen its original context. (The answers are all at the end of this chapter!)

Research focus: What is a classic?

Randall and Hardman argue that a classic text is 'a text with wide readership that has gained status over time and is considered a standard of its genre', while Geoff Fenwick (1990) maintained that a classic text 'represents the best in children's writing'.

Watson (1991) suggests that it is not enough to have stood the test of time: for a book to be determined a classic its qualities and appeals have to be transformed and adapted to new generations of readers – think of the many film and television adaptations some books have been through. *Alice's Adventures in Wonderland*, for instance, has been the source of at least thirty-five films (from silent movie in 1903, through Disney in 1951 to porn in 1976), two television series, a stage play, five video games, five theme park rides, two hit songs and two musical albums! Mark Twain described a classic book as 'a book which people praise but do not read'. However, to be a classic surely a book must be liked by children? Wilson and Abrahamson (1988) explored this idea in a study where a children's classic was defined as 'a book that has weathered at least one generation' (Jordan, 1976: 4) and is chosen by children in the next generation (Sayers, 1957).

Waterland, describing the value of reading classic texts to 5–7-year-olds, comments that 'the greatest value is certainly the new worlds that were opened for them, and the willingness with which they entered those worlds ... their language was enriched and their understanding of the familiar deepened ... most satisfyingly, there is the value that the children themselves found in the books, and that led them to want to go on exploring the worlds they found' (1989: 193).

As Carpenter (1985, p.1) stated: 'All children's books are about ideals. Adult fiction sets out to portray the world as it really is; books for children present it as it should be.'

When choosing anything written for a previous generation, however, there are usually issues of cultural and political sensitivity. Characters of any race other than white Caucasian are very rare in any book for children written in English much earlier than the end of the twentieth century, and references to other races and cultures are often derogatory or offensive. In the much-loved book by Frances Hodgson Burnett, *The Secret Garden*, for instance, the heroine Mary is deeply offended when the maid says to her, ' When I heard you was comin' from India I thought you was a black', and replies furiously, 'You don't know anything about natives! They are not people – they're servants who must salaam to you. You know nothing about India.' Now, the maid Martha is an uneducated Yorkshire girl, and Mary is a spoiled child, a product of the British Raj, and these characters would almost certainly have held those attitudes at the time when the book was written. In the course of the book, Mary's character improves and she becomes a kinder and more loving person. But how would you deal with that exchange of views in your classroom? Would you introduce it with an explanation of the historical context? Would you choose a simplified version? Or just choose another book altogether? Nicholas Tucker comments that most readers are 'quite capable of spotting such prejudices for what they are', and suggests that such stereotypes 'can provide an essential historical perspective for the origin and former popularity of various intolerant attitudes' (1981: 212). It is your decision as a teacher, and every case will need thought and discussion.

Books as diverse as *Peter Pan and Wendy* (J.M. Barrie), *Little House on the Prairie* (Laura Ingalls Wilder) and *Charlie and the Chocolate Factory* (Roald Dahl) have been criticised and bowdlerised because of their use of racially offensive language and/or insensitive treatment of disability issues. If choosing any book to share in your teaching, it's important to be aware of these aspects and to check carefully beforehand so that you can deal with them sensitively and satisfactorily. Even if you're only using part of a text, remember that there may be children who will then seek the full book out in the library. The following case study shows how a young teacher forestalled concerns about potentially sensitive areas in sharing a book with his class.

Case study: Oompa-Loompas

Faisal wanted to read Roald Dahl's *Charlie and the Chocolate Factory* with his Year 4 class, because it had been one of his own childhood favourites and he knew many children would have seen one of the film versions. However, he was aware of controversy surrounding the book, concerning both the Oompa-Loompa factory workers and the punishments received by four children in the story.

The Oompa-Loompas in Dahl's original story were a tribe of African pygmies. Dahl chose this characterisation because his factory workers had to be small enough to live their entire lives within the factory, and used to a very warm climate in which the chocolate river would stay molten. (His original publishers, interestingly, raised no problem because they saw the factory setting as 'in the Victorian tradition – a very English fantasy'.) When the implications of racism and slavery were first pointed out in a 1972 essay by Eleanor Cameron, Dahl changed the back-story of the Oompa-Loompas and made them light-skinned. They are cheerful and enjoy their situation. Faisal felt that, in the magical context of the story, the lives of the Oompa-Loompas would not attract comment or criticism from the children.

The punishments of the children, however, were an issue which he felt he ought to consider. A greedy and fat boy is apparently drowned in the chocolate river (but later rescued and squeezed out). A spoilt and avaricious girl is thrown out with the rubbish, a child addicted to chewing-gum is inflated and turned blue, and a television addict is shrunk to miniature size. All four suffer their fate through their own vice, in the tradition of Belloc's Cautionary Tales, and are left with permanent impairments. Faisal 'hot-seated' each of the four characters so that the class could ask them why they behaved as they did, and also did the same with Willy Wonka, who faced interrogation about his treatment of the children.

As follow-up work to this, the class wrote letters to the four children, suggesting how they might or should improve their lifestyle after their experience. At their suggestion, they also held a trial of Willy Wonka for cruelty to children, calling other characters as witnesses for the prosecution or defence. This led to interesting research into the legal process.

Many classic books which were not written with younger readers in mind start off with the protagonists' childhood. For example, consider Charles Dickens' *David Copperfield* or *Great Expectations*, Charlotte Brontë's *Jane Eyre*, or George Eliot's *The Mill on the Floss*. In each of these, the opening chapters deal with early childhood and are written with the child's perspective. Although a lot of the situations will of course be beyond modern children's experience, there are such scenes as young David imagining his new schoolmates from the sound of their names (in *David Copperfield*) or Maggie's sharing a jam-puff with her brother Tom (*The Mill on the Floss*) which will be familiar childhood experiences that can be shared. While few would suggest studying these texts in their entirety with any class below, perhaps, Year 9, an early introduction to these passages can help to make the whole book a less daunting prospect, as well as exposing children to both a more expanded use of language and a historical context.

One approach can be to give the children photocopies of the section of text to be read, and ask them to highlight any words that are unfamiliar. You can then discuss all the words they have found, and compile a class glossary before starting to read the passage in full.

The next case study suggests ways of making archaisms in a text accessible to modern children.

Case study: Wuthering Heights

Anna wanted to introduce her Year 6 class, who had been looking at childhood in Victorian times in their history lessons, to some nineteenth-century writing. She chose this passage from *Wuthering Heights*, by Emily Brontë, and explained that Heathcliff and Catherine had been out after dark to spy through the windows at the rich children in a nearby house. Heathcliff is telling the story to the housekeeper.

> Catherine (was) completely beaten in the race, because she was barefoot. You'll have to seek for her shoes in the bog to-morrow. We crept through a broken hedge, groped our way up the path, and planted ourselves on a flower-plot under the drawing-room window. The light came from thence; they had not put up the shutters, and the curtains were only half closed. Both of us were able to look in by standing on the basement, and clinging to the ledge, and we saw – ah! it was beautiful – a splendid place carpeted with crimson, and crimson-covered chairs and tables, and a pure white ceiling bordered by gold, a shower of glass-drops hanging in silver chains from the centre, and shimmering with little soft tapers. Old Mr. and Mrs. Linton were not there; Edgar and his sisters had it entirely to themselves. Shouldn't they have been happy? We should have thought ourselves in heaven! And now, guess what your good children were doing? Isabella – I believe she is eleven, a year younger than Cathy – lay screaming at the farther end of the room, shrieking as if witches were running red-hot needles into her. Edgar stood on the hearth weeping silently, and in the middle of the table sat a little dog, shaking its paw and yelping; which, from their mutual accusations, we understood they had nearly pulled in two between them. The idiots! That was their pleasure! to quarrel who should hold a heap of warm hair, and each begin to cry because both, after struggling to get it, refused to take it. We laughed outright at the petted things; we did despise them! When would you catch me wishing to have what Catherine wanted? or find us by ourselves, seeking entertainment in yelling, and sobbing, and rolling on the ground, divided by the whole room? I'd not exchange, for a thousand lives, my condition here, for Edgar Linton's at Thrushcross Grange.

- First, Anna handed out copies of the passage, so that the children could follow the story as they listened. She read the whole extract to the children, asking them to underline or highlight any words they didn't know. This led to explanation of items such as glass-drops, tapers and drawing-room, as well as unusual words like thence, mutual and petted, which some children understood and helped to explain. She then checked understanding by asking simple questions about the events, such as
  - Where were Cathy and Heathcliff?
  - What was the room like?
  - What were Edgar and Isabella doing?
  - What were they arguing about?
  - What did Heathcliff think of them?

- She then led on to ask what the children thought Catherine and Heathcliff's own house was like, and how Heathcliff showed his feelings for the Linton children.
- Next, she brought the class's own experiences in – had they ever peeped through a window from the outside? Did they compare their own homes with other people's?
- In groups of four, the children made up their own versions of the scene, using their own words to create both the Linton children's argument and a conversation between Catherine and Heathcliff. They acted these out for the rest of the class.

The term 'modern classics' is often used in two different senses; firstly, referring to the books written in the 'Second Golden Age' of children's literature, stretching roughly from 1950 to 1970, and secondly, to more recent books which have been so widely read that they seem to be acquiring the same position. Many of those in the former category – including the works of Joan Aitken, Rosemary Sutcliff, Roald Dahl, Philippa Pearce, Lucy M. Boston and Alan Garner – have been so frequently reprinted and/or adapted for film or television that classic status seems undeniable. Some of these have the advantage of timelessness – Clive King's *Stig of the Dump*, Aitken's Hanoverian fantasy sequence, or Sutcliff's historical novels, for instance. Also worth including here are Roger Lancelyn Green's retellings of classic stories – his *Tales of King Arthur* (1953), *Tales of the Greek Heroes* (1958) and *Tale of Troy* (1958) are among the clearest and most accessible versions of these tales, conveying all the epic excitement and character for younger readers. Other books from the 1950s and 1960s may need a bit of explanation for today's children. For instance, to take one of the best-known, *Tom's Midnight Garden* by Philippa Pearce, the concept of being sent away into quarantine for measles (and indeed, of measles itself!) is no longer a familiar one, and while it was possible in 1958 for an old lady to have grown up in Victorian times, it isn't now.

Books for younger children are often not rooted in any definite time, and so age less obviously. Maurice Sendak's *Where the Wild Things Are* appeared in 1963 and has never been out of print; Raymond Briggs' *The Snowman* came in 1978; even Eric Carle's *The Very Hungry Caterpillar* is more than fifty years old, and as such might be considered to have become a classic. In *The Tiger who Came to Tea* by Judith Kerr, although the milkman and the boy who delivers the groceries are historical details, the excitement of the story and the thrill of going out in the evening with a coat over your nighty continue to enthral.

Research focus: Swallows and Amazons

In 2011, Fiona Waller and Alison Maine set up an investigation into how adults and children respond to and engage with a classic children's text. They used

Arthur Ransome's *Swallows and Amazons*, the first in a series of stories about a group of children enjoying sailing, camping and imaginative adventures in the Lake District. All the adults involved, whose ages ranged from 28 to 78, had read the book as children; all the children were from Year 6 and were reading it for the first time. The authors commented that 're-reading is often contrasted with first reading and considered to be focused on interpretation rather than pleasure; but in working with adults returning to a childhood text, there is also an element of nostalgic enjoyment and engagement to be explored' (Maine and Waller, 2011: 5) and took this into account when comparing the two groups' reactions.

In brief, the children had engaged most with the adventurous and exciting incidents in the story, had identified most strongly with the two youngest characters, and not liked the descriptive passages. They were happy to admit that they sometimes skipped both the passages involving nautical jargon and descriptions, but this had not impaired their following of and immersion in the story. Some of the adults admitted to doing the same thing, but they were more ready to persist and get to the parts of the story they remembered liking best. The authors comment that 'Understanding of textual detail can be set aside as long as a coherent sense of the story is not compromised' (Maine and Waller, 2011: 11).

Although there was a clear socio-cultural gap between the children in the story (privileged, privately educated and enjoying freedoms few parents would grant today) and the readers, both adults and children had engaged fully with the text and the authors' final comment was that 'Hearing readers of all ages respond to, and delight in, the adventures and imagination of Titty, Roger, John and Susan demonstrates the power of an engaging read, and how some narratives and themes are timeless' (Maine and Waller, 2011: 18). Perhaps this is a good test for a true classic?

Discussion point

One of your colleagues is keen to use Enid Blyton's *Magic Faraway Tree* books as a class reader, because he loved this series as a child. He feels strongly that a teacher who loves a book can share this with a class more enthusiastically, and engage the children's interest and excitement better, than when reading a book at another's suggestion. He points out that the Faraway Tree series is frequently cited on lists of favourite books and childhood classics, such as the Book Trust's list of best books for children (Book Trust, 2021), and says he is looking forward to introducing children to the idea of different worlds which can be reached through climbing a magic tree. Some colleagues raise objections to this plan. What would your reaction be to discussion of the following points?

- Enid Blyton's writing is often cited as being racist, sexist or conveying old-fashioned attitudes – will the books cause offence?
- Blyton's style is very simple in construction, with a limited and undemanding vocabulary and a lot of exclamation marks – how will this help children develop their own writing styles?
- In earlier editions of the book, the four children – Joe, Beth, Frannie and Rick – are called Jo, Bessie, Fanny and Dick. If children find these names (which they may well do, as many adults still have copies of their childhood books), how would you explain the changes?
- How will the children benefit from reading this book together?

Having considered these points, would you advise your colleague to go ahead with his choice?

Today's best-sellers are, perhaps, too young to pass judgement on. Harry Potter, the Wimpy Kid, Horrid Henry – will they still be read and loved in 40 years' time? Longevity can be regarded, most would agree, as an essential requirement for a classic. However popular a book, writer or series is, we should wait and see whether it is still loved by a second generation before using the c-word!

Activity

Having read this chapter, make a list of ten books you would nominate as 'classics to be read before you're 11'. Then look at your list. What criteria did you use? Are they the same books that you named in the list you made at the beginning of the chapter? Maybe there are books you have always felt you ought to have read, but haven't yet! If you had to shortlist and eliminate some books, think about why you made those choices.

If your school literacy co-ordinator asked you why you had chosen one of these books to read in class, what would you say?

The Internet offers many lists of 'twenty, or fifty, or a hundred, classic books for children'. Compare your list with some of these. And when you find a book you are not familiar with – get hold of it and read it!

Learning outcomes review

By reading this chapter, you have:

- Considered what is meant by classic children's literature
- Identified some texts regarded as classic children's literature
- Considered how we define a classic

- Thought about why we read classic books with children
- Understood and critiqued the 'Golden Age' of children's books
- Reflected on the issue of modern classics
- Considered how we can introduce adult classics to children

Questions for discussion

- What do you consider counts as classic children's literature?
- Are there any examples of recent texts which you would consider already to be classics?
- How would you deal with language and ideas in older classic texts which may now be regarded as unacceptable?

Answers to the allusions

- I wandered, lonely as a cloud – *The Daffodils*, by William Wordsworth
- Grinning like a Cheshire Cat – the Cheshire Cat appears in Carroll's *Alice's Adventures in Wonderland*
- Time for a little something – *Winnie the Pooh*, by A.A. Milne
- Do as you would be done by – Mrs. Doasyouwouldbedoneby is in Kingsley's *The Water Babies*

For your bookshelf

A few more classic books, not mentioned in the chapter, to enhance your class's horizons.

Andersen, Hans, *Fairy Tales*.
All children should have the chance to read these classics – *The Snow Queen* and *The Little Mermaid* before Disney redesigned them, and many others.

Jansson, Tove (1945–1991) *Moomin* books.
The Moomins are creatures of no recognisable species or time. They live in a mysterious valley somewhere in Finland, with a huge sense of hygge. Their many adventures are filled with strong characterisation and a lot of humour. Strange events and magical happenings are frequent, but the overwhelming values are the strength of family and friendship.

Juster, N. (1961) *The Phantom Tollbooth*. New York: Epstein & Carroll.
The story of Milo, initially a bored boy who sees no point in much of life, who goes through a strange tollbooth that appears in his bedroom into a fantastic world full of wordplay and humour. The story is an adventure, as Milo sets out to rescue the princesses Rhyme and Reason, but is so full of puns, jokes and subtle wordplay that there

is more to be found on every reading. An enriching read, with some wisdom thrown in: 'You must never feel badly about making mistakes', explained Reason quietly, 'as long as you take the trouble to learn from them. For you often learn more by being wrong for the right reasons than you do by being right for the wrong reasons.'

Kipling, R. (1902) *Just So Stories*. London: Macmillan.
The classic fantasy stories explaining how animals obtained some of their features. Some of the attitudes and ideas may need explaining for modern children, but the humour and the pleasure of the language last well.

Lewis, C.S. (1950–1956) *Chronicles of Narnia*. London: Bodley Head.
Sometimes criticised for their Christian subtext, these books are nevertheless beloved, exciting and filled with humour. If you have concerns about the religious element, try *The Voyage of the Dawn Treader* or *The Silver Chair* from the middle of the series.

Milne, A.A. (1926) *Winnie the Pooh* and (1928) *The House at Pooh Corner*. London: Methuen.
If you're teaching in KS1, don't forget these! Children who have only ever seen the Disney films deserve to be introduced to the humour and style of the originals. (Quotations allegedly from the books have become so widespread that they seem to be part of national consciousness; however, the majority of these are totally spurious.)

Nesbit, E. (1902–1906) *Five Children and It, The Phoenix and the Carpet, The Story of the Amulet*. London: T. Fisher Unwin.
All Nesbit's children's books are of classic status – this trilogy in particular has a datelessly realistic family encountering first the stroppy Psammead, then the egocentric Phoenix, in magical adventures that often cause them problems.

Norton, M. (1952) *The Borrowers*. London: J.M. Dent (and sequels).
Miniature worlds have a perennial fascination, and these stories of the little people who live at first under the floorboards, then in a variety of other places, continue to charm. Recent film and television adaptations have kept them very much in circulation. (Studio Ghibli's *Arrietty* is a wonderful version.)

Bibliography

Aitken, J. (1962) *The Wolves of Willoughby Chase*. London: Jonathan Cape.
Barrie, J.M. (1911) *Peter Pan and Wendy*. London: Hodder & Stoughton.
Briggs, R. (1978) *The Snowman*. London: Hamish Hamilton.
Brontë, C. (1847) *Jane Eyre*. London: Smith, Elder & Co.
Brontë, E. (1847) *Wuthering Heights*. London: Thomas Cautley Newby.
Burnett, F.H. (1911) *The Secret Garden*. London: Heinemann.
Carle, E. (1969) *The Very Hungry Caterpillar*. London: Hamish Hamilton.
Dahl, Roald (1964) *Charlie and the Chocolate Factory*. London: George Allen & Unwin.
Defoe, D. (1719) *Robinson Crusoe*. London: W. Taylor.
Dickens, C. (1850) *David Copperfield*. London: Bradbury & Evans.
Dickens, C. (1861) *Great Expectations*. London: Chapman & Hall.
Eliot, G. (1860) *The Mill on the Floss*. London: William Blackwood & Sons.

Grahame, K. (1908) *The Wind in the Willows*. London: Methuen.
Green, R.L. (1953) *Tales of King Arthur*. London: Puffin.
Green, R.L. (1958) *Tales of the Greek Heroes*. London: Puffin.
Green, R.L. (1958) *The Tale of Troy*. London: Puffin.
Kerr, J. (1968) *The Tiger Who Came to Tea*. London: HarperCollins.
King, C. (1963) *Stig of the Dump*. London: Puffin.
Kingsley, C. (1863) *The Water-Babies*. London: Macmillan & Co.
Kipling, R. (1899) *Stalky & Co*. London: Macmillan & Co.
Lamb, C. and Lamb, M. (1807) *Tales from Shakespeare*. London.
Pearce, P. (1958) *Tom's Midnight Garden*. Oxford: Oxford University Press.
Potter, B. (1901) *The Tale of Peter Rabbit*. London: Frederick Warne & Co.
Ransome, A. (1930) *Swallows and Amazons*. London: Jonathan Cape.
Sendak, M. (1963) *Where the Wild Things Are*. London: Harper & Row.
Sewell, A. (1877) *Black Beauty*. London: Jarrold & Sons.
Sherwood, Mrs. (1818) *The History of the Fairchild Family*. London: Printed for J. Hatchard.
Swift, J. (1726) *Gulliver's Travels*. London: Printed for Benj. Motte.
Wilder, L.I. (1938) *Little House on the Prairie*. New York: Harper.

References

Book Trust (2021) *Best books for 6–8 year olds*. Available at: https://www.booktrust.org.uk/booklists/1/100-best-books-6-8/ (accessed 22 September 2021).

Carpenter, H. (1985) *Secret Gardens: The Golden Age of Children's Literature*. London: George Allen & Unwin.

Chiles, A. (2021) What speed reading has taught me about taking my time, *The Guardian*, 10 February. Available at: https://www.theguardian.com/commentisfree/2021/feb/10/what-speed-reading-has-taught-me-about-taking-my-time (accessed 17 February 2022).

Department for Education (DfE) (2011) *Teachers' Standards: Guidance for school leaders, school staff and governing bodies* (updated 2013 and 2021). London: DfE. Available at: https://www.gov.uk/government/publications/teachers-standards (accessed 16 February 2022).

Department for Education (DfE) (2013) *The National Curriculum in England: Key Stages 1 and 2 framework document*. London: DfE. Available at: https://www.gov.uk/government/publications/national-curriculum-in-england-primary-curriculum (accessed 30 July 2021).

Fenwick, G. (1990) *Teaching Children's Literature in the Primary School*. London: David Fulton.

Jordan, A. (1976) *Children's Classics*, 5th edn. Boston, MA: The Horn Book.

Locke, J. (2020) Locke's Thoughts Concerning Education, in A.L. Richards (ed.) *Philosophy of Education*. EdTech Books. Available at: https://edtechbooks.org/philosophy_of_education/locke_1693 (accessed 22 September 2021).

Lurie, A. (1990) *Not in Front of the Grown-Ups*. London: Cardinal.

Maine, F.A. and Waller, A.F. (2011) Swallows and Amazons Forever: How adults and children engage in reading a classic text, *Children's Literature in Education*, 42 (4): 354–371.

Randall, E. and Hardman, A. (2002) *A–Z of Key Concepts in Primary English*. London: Learning Matters.

Sayers, F.C. (1957) Books that enchant: What makes a classic?, *NEA Journal*, 48: 9–11.
Solzhenitsyn, A. (1970) *Nobel Lecture in Literature 1970*. Available at: https://www.nobelprize.org/prizes/literature/1970/solzhenitsyn/lecture/ (accessed 22 September 2021).
Tucker, N. (1981) *The Child and The Book*. Cambridge: Cambridge University Press.
Waterland, L. (1989) *Apprenticeship in Action*. Stroud: Thimble Press.
Watson, V. (1991) What Makes a Children's Classic, *Books for Keeps*, issue 71, November. Available at: https://booksforkeeps.co.uk/article/what-makes-a-childrens-classic/ (accessed 22 September 2021).
Wilson, P.J. and Abrahamson, R.F. (1988) What children's literature classics do children really enjoy?, *The Reading Teacher*, 41 (4): 406–411.

8 Poetry

"Poetry is the best words in the best order."

– Samuel Taylor Coleridge

Learning outcomes

By reading this chapter, you will develop your understanding of:

- What children need to understand about poetry
- Some of the challenges you face when you teach poetry
- Some approaches to teaching poetry

Link to the Teachers' Standards

3. Demonstrate good subject and curriculum knowledge

- have a secure knowledge of the relevant subject(s) and curriculum areas, foster and maintain pupils' interest in the subject, and address misunderstandings
- demonstrate a critical understanding of developments in the subject and curriculum areas, and promote the value of scholarship
- demonstrate an understanding of, and take responsibility for, promoting high standards of literacy, articulacy and the correct use of standard English, whatever the teacher's specialist subject

(DfE, 2011: 11)

Link to the National Curriculum

Pupils should be taught to:

- develop positive attitudes to reading and understanding of what they read by:
  - preparing poems and play scripts to read aloud and to perform, showing understanding through intonation, tone, volume and action

- discussing words and phrases that capture the reader's interest and imagination
- recognising some different forms of poetry [for example, free verse, narrative poetry]

(Years 3 and 4 Statutory Requirements, DfE, 2013: 35–36)

Ask any class – how many paragraphs from your favourite book do you know by heart? And then, how many lyrics of your favourite songs? It's easy to predict which will be the larger category. The rhymes and rhythms of poetry embed themselves into the memory without effort, and remain there for years. We consciously learn things by remembering little rhymed mnemonics, and the youngest of children often learn their favourite stories through rhymes. A small child who can't yet recognise the words on the page will be quick to correct you if you read a word wrong in *The Gruffalo* (Julia Donaldson) or *Goodnight Moon* (Margaret Wise Brown)!

In 1987, *Teaching Poetry in the Secondary School: An HMI view* was published. This highly influential pamphlet was a passionate argument for the central place of poetry in the secondary English curriculum. It argued:

> Poetry matters because it is a central example of the use human beings make of words to explore and understand. Like other forms of writing we value, it lends shape and meaning to our experiences and helps us to move confidently in the world we know and then to step beyond it.
>
> (HMI, 1987 quoted in Ofsted, 2007: 6)

How many of these do you recognise?

In fourteen hundred and ninety-two
Columbus crossed the ocean blue.

Sixteen hundred and sixty-five
The plague left hardly any alive
Sixteen hundred and sixty-six
London burned to ash and sticks.

Red sky at night, shepherd's delight,
Red sky in the morning, shepherd's warning

Thirty days has September,
April, June and November,
All the rest have thirty-one
Except for February alone,
Which has just twenty-eight days clear
And twenty-nine in each leap year.

And if you ask people to name a spelling rule this will usually be the one they come up with, even though it is not a very good rule and has lots of exceptions:

> i before e except after c

Can you think of others?

It is easy to see why looking at and sharing poetry can have an important place in the primary classroom. And yet it is often regarded with trepidation by many teachers, and the idea of poetry is regarded with hostility by some pupils. While it is hard to find definitive reasons for these attitudes, this chapter will try to show the importance of including poetry in the range of literature in your classroom, and suggest various ideas for teaching and studying it with a class.

Research focus: Teachers' knowledge of poetry

Ofsted's survey of schools in 2006/7 concluded: 'Many teachers, especially in the primary schools visited, did not know enough about poetry and this was reflected in the limited range of poems studied. Classic poems and poems from other cultures were rarely studied and too many of the poems chosen lacked sufficient challenge' (Ofsted, 2007: 4).

Ofsted also concluded that the quality of feedback on poetry writing was reduced by weaknesses in teachers' subject knowledge.

Cremin et al. (2008), investigating teachers' knowledge of poets, found that when asked to name 'six good poets', 58 per cent of the respondents named two, one or no poets, 22 per cent named no poets at all, and only 10 per cent named six poets. The poets named were a very restricted list, overwhelmingly of twentieth-century white males. Michael Rosen was the most frequently mentioned, followed by Allan Ahlberg and Roger McGough. Benjamin Zephaniah was the only Black poet to receive a significant number of nominations, Edward Lear and Christina Rossetti the only pre-twentieth-century names, and very few women poets at all – Grace Nicholls and Christina Rossetti scraped into the last two places of the top twenty poets named. Teresa Cremin and her colleagues comment that 'Whilst this is a matter of concern, it may reflect trends in anthologising and in the world of poetry more generally' (Cremin et al., 2008: 454).

Most children will come into the primary classroom with some knowledge of nursery rhymes and songs, and will be able to join in with the rhymes at the ends of lines, even if they don't know the whole verse. First creative coinings and nicknames are often founded on rhyme: silly billy, Rosy-posy, teeny-weeny, stinky-pinky, easy peasy lemon-squeezy. The fun of rhyme seems to be universal, and is something we can build on as a starting point and help develop to a greater depth as we look at poems in the classroom.

Ofsted's 2007 report found that the ten poems most read in primary schools were:

> 'The Highwayman' (Alfred Noyes)
>
> 'On the Ning Nang Nong' (Spike Milligan)
>
> 'Jabberwocky' (Lewis Carroll)
>
> 'The Owl and the Pussycat' (Edward Lear)
>
> 'From a Railway Carriage' (R L Stevenson)
>
> 'The Listeners' (Walter de la Mare)
>
> 'The Magic Box' (Kit Wright)
>
> 'The Sound Collector' (Roger McGough)
>
> From *Revolting Rhymes* (Roald Dahl)
>
> 'Dog in the Playground' (Allan Ahlberg)
>
> (Ofsted, 2007: 13)

How many of these do you know? Are you surprised by anything on the list?

It's clear that many teachers choose humorous poems, or ones which have a strong narrative story-line. It is certainly noticeable from the survey mentioned above and from this list, that the poets familiar to teachers are those whose main output is light and humorous. This is understandable, because these are the poems we can be confident the children will enjoy and understand. All the examples except *The Magic Box* have strong rhythms and rhyme schemes which give a good framework for imitative writing by children. However, this list does not reflect fully the National Curriculum criteria. In particular, Ofsted commented, 'good quality classic poems and poems from different cultures and traditions are missing. Furthermore, too few of these poems are genuinely challenging or connect with the direct experience of primary pupils' (2007: 13). We need, then, to find opportunities to extend our repertoires with more thought-provoking material.

Activity

Most definitions of poetry agree that it is about feelings and ideas, often connected with emotion and beauty. Think of such phrases as 'the view was sheer poetry' or 'the dance was poetry in motion'. In a radio broadcast on BBC Children's Hour in 1941, a speaker announced that he was not awarding a prize to any of the 2,000 entries in a poetry competition because 'they were verse – and verse is not automatically poetry' (King-Hall, 2021). Verse is defined in terms of rhyme and rhythm; many poems, of course, also have these qualities, but also evoke some kind of emotional response.

Look again at the list above. All of these poems are readily available on the Internet – take the time to find and read any with which you're not familiar. Which do you think qualify as poems, by this standard? Few people, probably, would argue that reading Milligan's *On the Ning Nang Nong* is a deeply moving experience. So why would you read it in class? Perhaps because it makes children laugh – and it is always worth being in control of the laughter in your classroom. Or perhaps because the structure makes it so easy to learn, so that children who would say they 'can't learn anything by heart' can gain in confidence?

Poetry has been defined in many different ways. One of the best-known definitions comes from Samuel Taylor Coleridge, who said in 1827 that 'Poetry is the best words in the best order' (quoted in *Table Talk* by his nephew), but nearly all definitions agree that poetry is about emotional response – the poet's response to a situation, shared with the reader. Reading or hearing a good poem should have an impact on a reader; ideally, the reaction sometimes defined as the 'Wow factor'. So when you want to introduce a poem, it can be a good idea to read it aloud, or watch the author reading it on YouTube, first, and ask the class how it made them feel. Find out which bits they liked or remembered best, or maybe what they thought the poet wanted us to feel. These are the important things. Later on in your study, you can come on to questions like the ones Ofsted found repeated endlessly on poetry worksheets: 'How many lines does it have? Which lines rhyme? List all the words that rhyme. How many syllables are there in each line? Can you find an example of: simile, metaphor, personification and onomatopoeia?' (Ofsted, 2007: 8). Try not to do this kind of dissection with every poem you read, though, or it makes reading poems a mechanical exercise instead of an imaginative one. If you take an old clock to pieces, you might understand the mechanism better, but it won't tell the time any more; or, to put it another way, all the ingredients of an ice-cream sundae set out neatly on a tray are never going to get the same 'Wow' as when they are all piled up with a strawberry on top!

Research focus: Children and young people's reading in 2020 before and during lockdown

The National Literacy Trust (NLT) surveys children's reading habits annually. The 2020 survey ended the week before lockdown in March, with schools closing for all but children of key workers and those deemed most vulnerable. The survey was the most popular to date, with 58,346 children and young people aged 9 to 18 from 315 schools in the UK participating between January and March 2020. The changed environment led the NLT to approach participating schools again to survey pupils while they were mostly staying at home, and 4,141 pupils aged 8 to 18 from 51 schools took part in an online survey between May and early June 2020.

The researchers found that 'more children and young people said that they enjoyed reading more and also read more during lockdown compared with before the start of the pandemic' (Clark and Picton, 2020: 14). When the results were analysed by type of materials read, it was noticeable that poetry was the literature showing the lowest increase in popularity: 11 per cent of respondents saying that they had read more on paper, 20.5 per cent saying they had read more online and 68.5 per cent saying that they had not read any more than they had before the lockdown. While this does not give a wholly negative picture, it does suggest that we can and should do more to encourage the idea that poetry is a part of our literature environment, not something kept in a separate compartment.

The Centre for Literacy in Primary Education suggests that you should 'Take time to drop poems into the school day, without any agenda to analyse or answer questions about them' (CLPE, 2017: 4). The educationalist Edward Blishen, in his autobiographical book *Roaring Boys*, describes a colleague on a snowy morning striding into the room and declaiming Hardy's *Snow in the Suburbs* ('Every branch big with it, Bent every twig with it ...'). Allan Ahlberg's *Colin* (in *Please Mrs Butler*), with a substitution of name as appropriate, can be used very effectively to disarm a potential complaint or classroom moan. You may find it worth learning that one, and one or two others, by heart, just so that you can come out with them impromptu. Thomas Hood's *November* or Ogden Nash's *Winter Song* could be two more useful ones to know.

Looking at two poems side by side can also make a great lesson, for Year 5 or Year 6 classes, as an exercise in looking for similarities and differences between styles and ideas. Try Kit Wright's *The Roller in the Woods* with Kipling's *The Way Through The Woods* – both ideas of forgotten or abandoned places. Or Brian Patten's *The Geography Teacher* with A.A. Milne's *The Island*, or Alfred Noyes' *The Old Grey Squirrel*, for the charm and romance of distant locations.

Poems can be a great way to introduce unfamiliar words and sounds just for the sheer pleasure of them – in fact, there is a classic poem *Romance* by Walter Turner, written in 1916, telling how the poet's imagination was seized by the sounds of the names 'Chimborazo, Cotopaxi, Popocatepetl.' (These are the names of three mountains in South and Central America, but it is just the magical sounds of the names which have captivated the poet.) The case study below shows how one teacher set out to encourage the love of enriched vocabulary in her class.

Case study: John Masefield's *Cargoes* as a stimulus for creative writing

Jasmine wanted to give her Year 6 class a chance to meet and use enriched vocabulary. She decided to use John Masefield's *Cargoes* as a stimulus for promoting some creative writing. She started by telling them the title of the poem, and asking what they thought a poem called *Cargoes* might be about. When the idea that it would be about the things carried by ships was established, she gave a copy of the poem to each child, and told them that they would find some very unusual words in it. Jasmine had prepared the sheet with a glossary of words such as quinquireme, isthmus, amethysts and moidores, and also a simple world map showing Nineveh, the Tropics and other places mentioned. She then showed the YouTube clip of Joanna Lumley reading the poem at https://www.youtube.com/watch?v=zD5sZdTtjJE.

The class discussed the poem: several had liked the long unfamiliar words, and the lists of exotic goods. Most of the children had picked up the idea that the ships mentioned were historical. Jasmine asked them what other kinds of ships Masefield might have written about, either modern or historical: the class came up with ideas from cruise ships and pirate ships to container ships and even airliners, as these have replaced shipping in so much international travel and transport. These ideas were all shared on the board, and the children contributed ideas as to what cargo each might be carrying. One boy commented that there are lots of long, complicated words in the first two verses of Masefield's poem, while in the last verse he uses short words, and the reasons why he might have done this were discussed. Jasmine then asked the children to work in pairs and create new stanzas for the poem, choosing a different type of ship. As they drafted, she encouraged them to notice the rhymes (which many had not spotted) and the structure of Masefield's writing. When each pair was satisfied with their production, they typed them up on the computer with decorations or illustrations, and printed them out for a classroom display.

From this case study we can see how the sounds of words can charm and delight, even if the meaning is not known. Poetry gives the opportunity to stop and look at unusual word choices in a way that we don't always have time for when reading prose.

Many older poems have refrains, which may be nonsense syllables giving a song-like structure (*hey nonny no, hey nonny no*) or repeated phrases. Look at repetition with your class – for instance, in Noyes' *The Highwayman*, lines are repeated (The highwayman came riding, riding, riding, The highwayman came riding up to the old inn door) and the third stanza is repeated as the last. The real events of the beginning of the poem are repeated by ghostly figures at the end, and the repetition emphasises this. Again, it's a trick that wouldn't work so well in a story. Take the time to look at longer narrative poems and ballads with your class, and talk about whether the story would be as effective if told in prose.

Poems don't have to stick to the same structure all the way through, either. Read Robert Browning's *The Pied Piper of Hamelin* aloud and see how the length of lines and the rhyme schemes vary to suit the pace of the story, from the formal beginning:

> Hamelin Town's in Brunswick,
> By famous Hanover city;
> The river Weser, deep and wide,
> Washes its wall on the southern side;

through the rhythm of the piper's appearance:

> And he himself was tall and thin,
> With sharp blue eyes, each like a pin,
> And light loose hair, yet swarthy skin,
> No tuft on cheek nor beard on chin,
> But lips where smiles went out and in –
> There was no guessing his kith and kin!

then the description of the vermin:

> Great rats, small rats, lean rats, brawny rats,
> Brown rats, black rats, grey rats, tawny rats,
> Grave old plodders, gay young friskers,
> Fathers, mothers, uncles, cousins,
> Cocking tails and pricking whiskers,
> Families by tens and dozens –

The poetic form adds to the drama of the story.

Activity

Most people would think of poetry as automatically falling under the wing of teaching English – but can it have a place in other subjects? Not much, in the full sense of analysing structure and emotion, but there is certainly a place for rhyme and rhythm across the curriculum. Did you first learn the alphabet with a song? Most of us did. Think back to the mnemonic rhymes at the beginning of this chapter. Your class might enjoy helping to make up new ones for different subjects. How about:

> Flowers and trees and all our plants
> All need five things, you know:
> Light and water, air and food,
> And space in which to grow.

(Year 3 Science)

Or:

> If it's pointy like the toe of a boot
> We say an angle is acute;
> But if it's floppy, wide and loose,
> Then we say that it's obtuse.
>
> (Year 4 Maths)

The great thing about doing these is that often, the sillier they are the better the class will remember them! Take a look at the curriculum you are delivering – especially the facts which children are expected to recognise and recall. Have a go at making up some rhymes for yourself, which could be the start of a classroom display.

A very useful verse form for this, especially if you're looking at the History curriculum, is the clerihew. A clerihew is a four-line poem of which the first line is usually the subject's name, and which usually includes at least one fact about her or his life; two of the best-known examples are:

> Sir Christopher Wren
> Said, 'I am going to dine with some men,
> If anyone calls,
> Say I am designing St. Paul's.

and

> Sir Humphrey Davy
> Abominated gravy;
> He lived under the odium
> Of having discovered sodium.

What could you do with, say, Julius Caesar? Alfred the Great? Rosa Parks? Or Mary Seacole?

Another benefit of using such tactics across the curriculum is that you can exploit the pleasure which children find in appreciating the fun of rhyme and rhythm. If you only ever meet these ideas when you are 'doing' a poem, they can easily come to seem less interesting.

The National Curriculum prescribes that right from Year 1 pupils should learn 'some' poems by heart, and by Year 6 they should learn 'a wider range' by heart. There is no definition of how many poems this should be, or a statutory canon of what should be included. As with everything in classrooms, some pupils will enjoy the challenge and others find it very challenging. There are many ways to make the task easier – reading a poem together, sharing it out so that each verse is read by one pair or small group, stopping before the end of a line so that the children can supply the last word. Working in groups can be a good exercise – make it fun, and make it a performance! Whether a child has learnt eight lines of doggerel, or all seventy verses of 'How Horatius kept the Bridge', the effort has been made and deserves an audience and some praise. Be ready to prompt if needed, and encourage the speaker to be clear and loud. Most children speaking poetry have a tendency to go too fast, perhaps in the effort to get to the end before they forget the words, so make sure that when reading you always model a good delivery which they can copy.

Sometimes children can feel constrained if the teacher introduces a poem to them, feeling that there are right and wrong ways to react. The case study below offers an idea for letting the children investigate new poems by themselves, without an initial reading.

Case study: Exploring different genres

Dan wanted his Year 5 class to look at different types of poetry. He chose a selection of different genres, and divided the class into groups. He explained that each group would be given three tasks – to write two or three short sentences explaining or introducing their poem, to choose and rehearse how they would present it to the class, and to choose three words which they felt summed up the mood of the poem. The tasks were discussed with the full class, and contributions of words which might be useful were all put on the whiteboard.

Each group had a different poem to study, with a variety of styles and moods being included. The poems were:

Mimi's Fingers by Mary O'Neill
The Betsy Street Booters by Allan Ahlberg (from *Friendly Matches*)
The Ghost Teacher by Allan Ahlberg (from *Heard it in the Playground*)
Man the Musicmaker by Roger McGough (from *Sky in the Pie*)
Autumn Song by Ted Hughes
Winter by Abbi Baker

When they had had time to prepare, Dan asked each group to introduce and perform their poems to the rest of the class. Most groups chose to share out lines or verses in turn, some using choral speaking effectively on some lines, some using mime or gesture to add dramatic effects. After each poem he asked the class what words they thought the group might have chosen for their poem. This gave an element of a game to the lesson, with the groups saying 'yes', 'no' or 'nearly' to suggestions. At the end of the lesson he asked the class which poem they had found most interesting, and which they'd liked best.

He felt that the children had reacted well to discovering their poems for themselves, without giving them an introduction, and were more ready in future to approach poetry with an open mind.

There are two 'bad' things which children, and many adults, do when reading poetry aloud. As a teacher, you can step in and help eliminate these faults. The first is to put on a 'poetry-reading voice'. If you've ever listened to poetry being read on the radio, you will recognise this concept. People who speak perfectly normally the rest of the time often adopt a semi-hushed tone and a slow and monotonous delivery as soon as a poem is in front of them. This tone is partly to blame for the impression so many have that poetry is something boring, arcane and semi-sacred. When you read a poem to your class, keep it as conversational as you can, and encourage them to do the same when reading or reciting.

The second fault to guard against is the tendency to stop at the end of every line. Take, for example, the poem frequently held up as the best-known and most frequently learnt in English schools, Wordsworth's 'The Daffodils'. How often have you heard, 'I wandered, lonely as a cloud', with the voice descending on 'cloud' as if it were the end of a sentence? But this is 'a cloud that floats on high –'. If you stop at the end of the first line, you then have the line 'That floats on high o'er vales and hills', which doesn't work as a free-standing phrase. If it wasn't set out as a poem, you wouldn't pause after 'cloud' – so don't let children get into the habit of not looking at punctuation! The carrying on of sense from one line to the next is called *enjambment* – linking, and occurs in many famous poems. One well-known example is from T.S. Eliot's *The Waste Land*:

> April is the cruellest month, breeding
>
> Lilacs out of the dead land, mixing
>
> Memory and desire, stirring
>
> Dull roots with spring rain.

If explaining this to a class, you could use the old punctuation puzzle:

> Caesar entered on his head
>
> A helmet on each foot
>
> A sandal in his hand he had
>
> His trusty sword to boot.

which makes no sense if read metrically (stopping at the end of each line) but can be made sense of with proper punctuation and pauses. (The answer is at the end of the chapter.)

Another pleasure of poetry in the classroom is, of course, the opportunities it can give for creative writing. The Centre for Literacy in Primary Schools reminds us that 'Wordplay is one of the most basic pleasures of poetry, giving the opportunity for playing games with language so that the shapes, sounds, and rhythms of words are enjoyed as well as their meaning' (CPLE, 2017: 10).

Younger children can enjoy creating acrostics, where the initial letters of each line spell out a word or name – for example:

Happy
Off to the seaside
Lots of fun,
I can't wait!
Dad, Mum and my brothers
All come too.
Yes! Nearly the end of term
Summer is great!

There is no need for rhyme, formal structure or even grammatical construction in an acrostic, so they are relatively easy to compose. Concrete poems, too, where the words are formed into the shape of the subject, are popular. The joy of the sounds of words can be enjoyed in many poems; Spike Milligan's *On The Ning Nang Nong* has already been mentioned – try also Allan Ahlberg's *Ping Pong Song* at https://clpe.org.uk/poetryline/poets/ahlberg-allan.

The case study below shows how a young teacher helped her Year 1 class to understanding and enjoyment of a poem.

Case study: Learning poetry by heart with Year 1

Kim wanted to help her Year 1 class enjoy Julia Donaldson's poem, *The Nut Tree* (in *Wriggle and Roar*). She had chosen this because it is fairly short and clear, with a strong rhyme and rhythm pattern, and because the class had recently been looking at 'Growing Things' and had planted seeds in pots in class. She also wanted the children to get used to the idea of learning by heart, so that they would be able to present the poem to the school in a class assembly.

First she read the poem to them, clearly and fairly slowly. She asked the children:

- What was that poem about?
- Did you like it?
- How did you know it was a poem?
- What happened at the end? (The poem, which tells of a nut growing into a tree, ends with the same line with which it begins – 'small, brown, hard, round.' – as a new nut falls from the tree.)

The class had all enjoyed and understood the poem, and recognised that it rhymed. Some had noticed that the last line was the same as the first, and one boy's comment was that 'it's like it's all ready to begin again'.

Kim then displayed the text on the whiteboard, but with the last word in every other line missing. She asked the children to see if they could remember the rhyming words to complete the lines, and read the poem through, stopping at each gap. As the right word was supplied, she filled in the gap. When the text was complete, the class read it aloud together. They then looked at each rhyme and made a collection of ideas of other words which have the same rhyme – so, for instance, with 'tree' and 'be' the class suggested see, we, sea, tea, free, and three.

They read the poem again, this time with hand actions from a closed fist as the nut, then a finger as the shoot, to arms waving for the grown tree. Kim then removed the text from the board and read just the first half of each line. Most of the children were able to finish the line off, speaking together. The next time she just gave alternate lines, and found many children could supply the whole of the couplet. At the end of the session, she asked if anyone thought they could say the whole poem. Three children managed completely – several others only needed one prompt.

The whole poem was used as a centrepiece for artwork in the classroom, so that the children would keep seeing it. At the class assembly they were able to recite the poem together without the script.

This case study shows how sharing a poem can not only give confidence to children for learning by heart and performing, but also tie in to their phonic and language development work.

In KS2, children can enjoy the discipline of counting syllables to compose haiku or cinquain verses. A haiku has seventeen syllables in three lines, arranged 5/7/5, and a cinquain has five lines with a syllable pattern 2/4/6/8/2. You can find many examples of these, and other poetic forms, on the CLPE website. Counting the syllables, and looking at how longer words break up into syllables, is an excellent way for children to look at the structure of words and see the individual morphemes within a word. As children structure these poems, they will learn to choose exactly the right words to express an idea concisely. With access to a good thesaurus, either paper or online, it can be an excellent exercise in vocabulary enrichment. And there are also limericks, tankas and many other forms to explore. However, be careful not to do this aspect of poetry to death – as mentioned earlier, it's easy to lose the pleasure of the poem when you get too concerned with the mechanics of it!

You don't need to go into lots of technical metrical analysis, which can be difficult and off-putting, at this stage – talking about 'feet' or 'beats' in a line is sufficient without introducing terms like *iambic pentameter*. The idea of *onomatopoeia* is likely to come up – for instance, when the horse's hooves go *tlot-tlot* in Noyes' *The Highwayman*, one of the poems cited by Ofsted as frequently read in KS2 classes. Some children may already be familiar with the word; its strange sound and structure usually make it popular and memorable.

(When there's a bang, a splash or a thump,

There is no need to fear,

There's nothing that should make you jump,

Just onomatopoeia!)

Poetry is an important part of literature, and an essential element of English Literature GCSE. This means that as children move up to secondary school, they will be regularly having poetry sessions in their English curriculum; those who already enjoy and feel at home with it will have an enormous advantage, and be more receptive to increasingly complex forms and ideas. By showing your class what an enormous range is out there, you can encourage a positive idea of poetry and extend your own love and interest along with theirs.

Learning outcomes review

By reading this chapter, you will have developed your understanding of:

- What children need to understand about poetry
- Some of the challenges you face when you teach poetry
- Some approaches to teaching poetry

Punctuation puzzle

Caesar entered; on his head, a helmet, on each foot a sandal. In his hand, he had his trusty sword to boot.

Questions for discussion

- What can poetry do that prose can't?
- What are the advantages of telling a story, or picturing a scene, in a poem?
- Why do some poems stick in the mind?
- How can you develop poetry in your school?

For your bookshelf

A few good anthologies will offer your class a wide range of subjects and styles, with something for everybody. Give time, when you can, for them to browse and find a favourite of their own.

Belloc, H. (1907) *Selected Cautionary Tales*. London: Puffin.
Classic and comical stories of, mostly, misbehaving children meeting awful fates. The rhymes are fun, the form easy to learn, remember and imitate!

Esiri, A. (ed.) (2016) *A Poem for Every Day of the Year*. London: Pan Macmillan.

A wide variety of 366 poems, some well-known favourites and some new, linked to the day and the season – specific events on key dates (like 1 April or 5 November) add interest.

Riddell, C. (ed.) (2020) *Poems to Save the World With.* London: Pan Macmillan.
Chris Riddell has illustrated his selections in this anthology and it is a pleasure to look at. Many of the poems are insightful and inspiring, with messages about taking care of each other and of the planet. It's an up-to-date selection, including some poems about the lockdown situation.

Anything by Michael Rosen.
Funny, lively narrative poems about childhood.

Waters, F. (ed.) (2020) *Tiger, Tiger, Burning Bright.* London: Nosy Crow.
Beautifully illustrated anthology, with poems for all age groups. The bright pictures will attract and engage, and the range of verses, from familiar classics to short verbal images from a wide range of cultures, will keep the pages turning.

Webb, K. (ed.) (1979) *I like This Poem.* London: Puffin.
This anthology was compiled from children's choices to celebrate the International Year of the Child. It is full of favourites, each with an introduction from a child who chose it, and is helpfully arranged in sections with suggested age-ranges.

Anything by Kit Wright.
Funny, rhythmic poems with lots of wordplay. There are a few thought-provoking, more serious poems in among the humour – *The Roller in the Woods*, for example, or *Useful Person.*

Bibliography

All poems referred to in the chapter are available from so many anthologies and websites that you will find them easily. Only specific books are listed here.

Ahlberg, A. (1983) *Please Mrs Butler.* London: Kestrel Books.
Ahlberg, A. (1989) *Heard it in the Playground.* London: Viking Kestrel.
Ahlberg, A. (2001) *Friendly Matches.* London: Viking.
Donaldson, J. (1999) *The Gruffalo.* London: Walker Books.
Donaldson, J. (2005) *Wriggle and Roar.* London: Pan Macmillan.
Eliot, T.S. (1922) *The Waste Land.* London: Faber & Faber.
McGough, R. (1983) *Sky in the Pie.* London: Puffin.
Wise Brown, M. (1947) *Goodnight Moon.* London: Harper.

References

Centre for Literacy in Primary Education (CLPE) (2017) *Poetry in Primary Schools: What we know works.* Available at: https://clpe.org.uk/research/poetry-primary-schools-what-we-know-works (accessed 17 February 2022).

Clark, C. and Picton, I. (2020) *Children and Young People's Reading in 2020 Before and During Lockdown*. London: National Literacy Trust. Available at: https://cdn.literacytrust.org.uk/media/documents/National_Literacy_Trust_-_Reading_practices_under_lockdown_report_-_FINAL.pdf (accessed 17 February 2022).

Cremin, T., Mottram, M., Bearne, E. and Goodwin, P. (2008) Exploring teachers' knowledge of children's literature, *Cambridge Journal of Education*, 38 (4): 449–464.

Department for Education (DfE) (2011) *Teachers' Standards: Guidance for school leaders, school staff and governing bodies* updated (2013 and 2021). London: DfE. Available at: https://www.gov.uk/government/publications/teachers-standards (accessed 16 February 2022).

Department for Education (DfE) (2013) *The National Curriculum in England: Key Stages 1 and 2 Framework Document*. Available at: https://www.gov.uk/government/publications/national-curriculum-in-england-primary-curriculum (accessed 30 July 2021).

Department for Education and Science (DfES) (2000) *Teaching Poetry in the Secondary School: An HMI view*. London: HMSO.

King-Hall, Commander Sir Stephen, quoted on BBC Radio 4 *Rewinder*, 6 March 2021.

Ofsted (2007) *Poetry in Schools: A survey of practice, 2006/07*. London: HMSO. Available at: https://dera.ioe.ac.uk/7075/8/Poetry_in_schools_(PDF_format)_Redacted.pdf (accessed 17 February 2022).

Creating children's literature with children

"I think this is a brilliant book because I helped write it! You will be engrossed in this story. Enjoy!:-)"

– Review of *The Wishroom* in Amazon

Learning outcomes

By reading this chapter, you will have considered:

- The importance of creating children's literature with children
- How teachers can develop children's understanding of and engagement with texts
- The value of stories and some simple ways of engaging children in writing them
- A range of possible writing activities
- Ways of 'publishing' children's writing

Link to the Teachers' Standards

3. Demonstrate good subject and curriculum knowledge

- demonstrate an understanding of and take responsibility for promoting high standards of literacy, articulacy and the correct use of standard English

4. Plan and teach well structured lessons

- promote a love of learning and children's intellectual curiosity
- contribute to the design and provision of an engaging curriculum

(DfE, 2011: 11)

Link to the National Curriculum

During years 5 and 6, teachers should continue to emphasise pupils' enjoyment and understanding of language, especially vocabulary, to support their reading and writing. Pupils' knowledge of language, gained from stories, plays, poetry, non-fiction and textbooks, will support their increasing fluency as readers, their facility as writers, and their comprehension.

(Upper Key Stage 2 – Years 5 and 6, DfE, 2013: 41)

In this chapter, we will explore ways in which teachers can work with children to create children's literature. We will look at some activities and pedagogical strategies which you might use in your own classroom and will consider how creating texts can help us to gain insights into authorship and the writing process, while encouraging discussion about children's literature.

We begin by exploring one end of the writing spectrum: production of a class novel. David Waugh has worked with children to publish two novels: *The Wishroom* (2017), which involved 45 children from 15 schools, and *Twins?* (2019), which involved 12 children in one school. For each novel, David wrote an opening which was shared and discussed with the children before they began to write. At various stages of the writing, David acted as scribe and drew upon children's ideas to move the story forward. *The Wishroom* is a single story which includes different children's experiences within the same setting. This involved planning a series of scenarios, including:

- Children's experiences of meeting and sharing a dormitory with others whom they had not previously met
- Having a banquet at which they could order any food they wanted
- Exploring a dark stately home at night
- Meeting a nun and a monk who granted each child a wish, in return for which they had to perform a good deed
- Taking part in a range of activities as part of a residential visit
- Experiencing their wish coming true
- Performing a good deed
- Parting company from new friends

The sequence and the events were modified as the story progressed over a series of weekly workshops, but the structure allowed children freedom to pursue their own ideas within a framework. They handwrote their sections and these were typed and corrected by David. Each workshop began by revisiting the writing produced at the previous one in preparation for the next stage. This approach seemed to work well and a final proof was made into a published novel, illustrated by the children and available through Amazon and other distributors. Parents, grandparents and teachers were invited to celebrate the publication with afternoon tea at a local hotel, readings from the children, and press photographs. However, when a school in West Durham asked David to work with children in a similar way, a slightly different approach was taken.

In the next section, you will find the opening to *Twins?*, which David wrote and shared with twelve Year 5/6 children. After reading the opening, please look at the activity and then the discussion.

Example: *Twins?*

CHAPTER 1

TWINS?

The noise was deafening, but my world seemed suddenly silent. A moment ago I had been surrounded by a cacophony of voices asking questions like, 'What can I get for 17p?' and 'Can I borrow 32p so I can get one of those rulers, please?' and 'Miss, Javed's pushing in!'

The museum shop was full of children, with a few harassed looking teachers and teaching assistants. Every now and then an adult voice could be heard saying something like, 'Right, St Joseph's children, you have two minutes left and then we have to leave. I told you you only had ten minutes before we went into the museum. You'll get longer when we've had our visit' or 'Brookbank children, you don't have to spend every penny you brought with you. Anyway, I want everyone in a line by the door in one minute'. The time constraints just seemed to make everyone louder, as a sea of blue sweat-shirted Y5 and 6 pupils tried to get served by the rather frazzled looking shop assistants.

But my attention had been taken away from the noise and the chaos around me. I was still holding a notepad with National Railway Museum on the cover, but I no longer tried to join the unruly queue at the till. Instead, I gazed intently at the mirror above the counter which was angled so that it showed every part of the museum shop. I was looking at my reflection, but what I saw disturbed me. My sweatshirt was blue – I looked down at it to confirm this, even though I knew everyone in my class was wearing the same school uniform. But it was dark blue, not the paler shade I could see in my reflection. And another thing, the badge on the front was brown and not red like the one I saw in the mirror.

I raised my hand to push my hair away from my forehead, but my reflection didn't move. I tried folding my arms, but the figure in the mirror remained still. I stared at the freckles which my classmates teased me about and at my fair hair, which my mother had insisted on combing that morning. Then I looked to my left and saw him. Somehow you can tell when someone is looking at you, even when you haven't been looking at them. Our eyes met. His mouth fell open and a look of surprise filled his face. This was quickly followed by an expression of puzzlement and wonder. We began to try to move towards each other, but the crowds of shoppers got in the way and before I could get to within five metres of him I heard Mrs Sadler's booming voice:

'Daniel Welton, please put that notebook back on the shelf. It's too late to buy it now. If we manage to get round the museum before the bus arrives, you can come back and buy it then.'

I turned to replace the notebook on the shelf behind me and then turned back to see my mysterious double, but he had gone.

All I saw was the backs of around thirty children in pale blue sweatshirts heading out of the shop as their teachers counted them and told them to line up in twos. I stepped towards the receding blue line and suddenly saw his face again as he turned to scan the shop. He mouthed a word which I thought was probably 'Mallard', and then held up one hand and spread his fingers while mouthing what was clearly the word 'five'. I paused to take this in, but Mrs Sadler's voice interrupted my thoughts, 'Come along, Daniel, this way!' Reluctantly, I joined the end of my class's line and we headed out of the shop and into the vast museum.

(Waugh et al., 2019: 1–2)

Activity

After reading the story opening to *Twins?,* consider what you might do with your class.

How could you take this forward?

You might read the story opening and then pose questions such as:

- Why are the boys so surprised to see each other?
- How would you react if you saw someone who looked just like you?

It is this speculation about what might happen next or how a situation arose which is one of the key attractions of fiction. By introducing unusual scenarios to children, we can not only engage their interest, but also put them in control of the storyline if we go on to write with them and enable them to write independently.

Twins? provided opportunities to discuss the process of writing a story, starting with where the initial idea came from. David explained, and acknowledged at the front of the published book, that he got the idea after reading Daphne du Maurier's adult novel *The Scapegoat*, in which two identical men meet by chance and go on to swap lives.

Discussion

The most adventurous, and time-consuming, next step would be to complete the story with your class. This might be done by children writing a continuation individually or in pairs or you could choose to write parts of the story with them, drawing on their ideas and acting as a scribe to model writing. If you take this route, you need to be aware of the importance of sustaining momentum and enthusiasm. You will need, in consultation with the children, to decide whether there is to be a single version of the story which everyone agrees upon, or if there will be a series of alternative versions. In producing *Twins?*, it quickly became evident that children had very different ideas about how the story might evolve. It was decided that it would be a pity to discount some of the ideas in order to produce a coherent single story and so each person, including David, wrote their own version. Two children worked together, while the other ten worked individually. The resulting book was published and presented at the school's end of year awards evening.

Both projects enabled children to gain insights into the writing process and emphasised the importance of editing and refining text, as well as making the written work engaging and interesting for readers. The writers were able to discuss key features of novels such as settings, characters and plot, and the importance of including cliffhangers at the ends of sections so that readers will want to read on. With both novels, children learned about the publishing process and the importance of careful editing and proof-reading. For each book the publisher sent a sample pre-publication copy for checking by the authors. In the case of *The Wishroom*, careful proof-reading of this copy led to the discovery of dozens of typographical errors and the misspelling of two children's names. (It should be noted that children wrote *The Wishroom* by hand and David typed up their efforts and corrected spelling and grammar but not content. It was a salutary task showing the children that the author of more than sixty books was capable of making so many mistakes.)

Such projects involve a lot of commitment and may not be possible for many teachers, so what other activities might be undertaken to develop children's understanding of literature and to encourage them to discuss it and share their opinions? In the next section, you will find some possibilities.

Developing children's understanding of literature

Settings

As we have seen elsewhere in this book, one of the joys of literature is the opportunity it provides to explore unfamiliar settings for stories: a magical kingdom, a dark and forbidding wood, a secret garden or a different time period. Many novels have more mundane settings, but we need to ask if children can relate to the setting of the story we are exploring. Through discussion, sharing images, perhaps online, and through talking about other stories, can we ensure that children feel comfortable about reading and writing about the setting we are focusing upon. In working on *Twins?* and *The Wishroom*, David visited and photographed places which could feature in the story and shared these images with the children. Children discussed the pictures, and vocabulary and phrasing were shared so that everyone had access to a developing word bank. The setting was chosen as being one which children might be familiar with: a school trip to a museum. The school was close to the National Railway Museum at York, so most children would have visited at least once. The opening setting of a busy museum shop would almost certainly be familiar to Year 5/6 children, as would the children's eagerness to spend their money. It is a common authorial device to start with the familiar and then introduce something unusual: in this case, the identical boys catching sight of each other.

Characters

There are many ways in which characters can be explored so that children can reflect on motivation and mood. A simple starting point can be to provide pairs of children with pictures or simply names of characters in the centre of a large piece of paper. They are then asked to make rapid notes on how characters are feeling, or what kind of person they might be. Discussion should be encouraged and the writing need not include sentences, but rather single words, phrases and brief descriptions. After a short burst of writing and talking, ideas can be shared by the class and the teacher can write some suggestions on the board, thereby enhancing everyone's vocabulary and providing correct spellings.

Another strategy for considering character is hot-seating, which involves one child taking on the role of a character and responding to people's questions in role. It is a good idea to give children who are to be in the hot seat time to prepare and to encourage them to answer in detail sometimes.

Some teachers use a technique known as 'word on the wall', which involves displaying pictures of names of characters and inviting children to add descriptions as a story progresses. If a story is being read to them, they might be given time at the end of an excerpt to write ideas on pieces of paper or Post-its and then put these on the wall. Again, this provides a word bank to support writing and gives teachers an opportunity to discuss vocabulary and address any spelling problems.

When writing with children, a useful strategy can be to create a bank of ideas and record these at the side of the board on which you will be writing, so that these notes can be drawn upon to create sentences. This is a technique which children might be encouraged to try in their independent writing, as it helps sustain momentum in writing by providing a word bank.

Plot

Writers, including the present authors, often begin a project with a wave of enthusiasm and a flurry of activity, only to find that this soon dissipates and they begin to suffer from what is sometimes termed *writer's block*. This can be frustrating and disheartening and is certainly something any teacher of writing will have seen in pupils. One way to mitigate this is to encourage note-making and storyboarding so that an outline of a story's plot is always available. Of course this can be modified as new ideas replace initial thoughts, but it does give a structure to fall back on when enthusiasm flags. This is a technique which older pupils are often encouraged to use in examinations – jot down a plan for each essay you will write while your revision is fresh in your mind. Then, if you run out of ideas, you have something to draw upon to get you going again.

So far, we have emphasised the value of cooperative discussion and writing, so it is worth pausing for a moment to consider some of the research which supports this approach.

Research focus: Cooperative working

Elisondo maintained that 'creative ideas and products always depend, in a certain way, on interaction with other people and culturally constructed and reconstructed knowledge' (2016: 195). In her view, creative thinking does not happen in a solitary vacuum but in a socially constructed way through interaction with others.

Knight and Mercer (2015) asserted that exploratory talk constituted 'reasoned discussion' and that collaboration leads to higher quality educational outcomes.

Kampylis and Berki (2014: 16) maintained that collaboration increases creative thinking and enables children to explore a wider range of perspectives.

This cooperation extends to teacher–pupil as well as pupil–pupil cooperation. Falconer et al. (2018) see learning as an interactive process where teachers model the creative process. The relationship here therefore is crucial. This modelling involves dialogue between teacher and learner, and support from the teacher for the learner.

The Durham Commission on Creativity and Education (2019: 66) identified the conditions necessary for high-quality teaching for creativity in schools and the learning environments that would facilitate this. Among these were:

- Opportunities to 'fail without fear', to be reflective, and to try again, thereby developing children's resilience
- A classroom culture tolerant of ambiguity, paradox and diverse points of view
- Pedagogies which encourage experimentation, multiple perspectives, persistence and collaboration

A wonderful example of how a teacher can model writing and engage children's interest is shown in the case study below. Author Michael Morpurgo describes how he became a writer by accident. When he was a primary school teacher, the part of the day which he and his pupils enjoyed most was the stories he read to them for the last half hour of each day. He enjoyed acting out the stories and making them engaging, and found his pupils enjoyed this too.

Case study: How Michael Morpurgo became a writer

Morpurgo relates how he began a book with his class on one occasion and found that they quickly became bored and restless. After discussing this with his wife, Morpurgo took her advice and decided to tell rather than read the story and found that the children were rapt as they listened. He went on to tell them stories each week, ending each day on a 'cliffhanger' and completing the stories on Friday afternoons. He describes how children related to the stories because they were *his* stories rather than ones from published books. In an interview he explained: 'There was a big reason ... I meant it. I meant every single word I was telling them. Why did I mean it? Because I'd made it up. I'd done it myself. And I wanted them to be drawn into this story.' (The interview is available at: https://www.godwinprimary.co.uk/michael-murpurgo-2/)

On one occasion, the headteacher observed Morpurgo telling a story and told him that he should write the stories down and bring them to her so that she could send them to a publisher friend. He duly did this and eventually became a highly successful author with more than 100 books in print.

Of course, we are not suggesting that all teachers who create stories for their classes will become famous authors, but there are lessons to be learned from Morpurgo's experiences. His and our own experiences of working in schools with stories we have created show that children can be fascinated by how we create narrative. Children often ask where ideas came from and especially enjoy hearing how a chance encounter or a visit to a place which they too have visited prompted an idea. While stories include elements of fantasy such as Jessica passing through a trapdoor into another world (in David Waugh's *Jessica's Other World*, 2016), they can also include experiences which readers can identify as familiar, such as going to school, arguing with siblings and playing games. Part of the appeal of the Harry Potter series is its school setting. Despite the strange curriculum and the elements of magic, readers can still relate to Hogwarts pupils' experiences of bullying, lessons and teachers they like and dislike, and the development of friendships. It is important to consider how familiar themes can be combined with extraordinary events if you decide to tell or write stories for your pupils.

A cautionary note from Hughes (2020: 116):

> When you create a text to use, you are offering it as an excellent example of what you expect from the pupils. It can also be used as a stimulus to provoke the children to express their own ideas. The reason this can be difficult is that you will be opening yourself up to possible criticism – the pupils may not appreciate the text and your colleagues might spot mistakes or issues with what you have created. Knowing that this might happen could put teachers off writing their own texts.

However, these potential disadvantages can actually be turned into advantages. By laying our writing open to constructive criticism, we can model what real writers go through as they hone and refine their texts. We might even show some examples of famous writers' drafting to illustrate the processes they went through as their prose or lyrics developed. Interesting drafts of famous adult novels can be found on *BBC Culture* (Anderson, 2020).

Besides, many teachers make deliberate mistakes when they write in front of children, to encourage them to spot the errors. And this strategy often enables us to 'get away with' unintentional errors by saying, 'Well done. I wondered if anyone would spot that!'

Why write for children?

There are, then, two main ways in which teachers might write for children. The first is to prepare text in advance of lessons and then share it, either or both by reading it aloud and by sharing it, perhaps via a whiteboard or sharing hard copies. Text written in advance can be checked and made accurate when appropriate. However, the second mode of writing for children, shared writing, may make teachers feel more vulnerable, since it involves creating text as children watch. Baker and Cremin (2018) suggest that such spontaneous composition offers little protection from emotional exposure. Nevertheless, shared writing can be developed so that, while the teacher is always the scribe, ideas can flow from the class as the writing develops. This can reduce pressure on teachers anxious about children's reactions to their text, and also provides opportunities to model not only the actual writing but also the thinking processes behind it. Teachers and pupils can 'think aloud' as they try out vocabulary, spellings and phrasing and use of reference sources can be included to check on transcriptional elements. However, it is worth noting Cremin and Baker's assertion that:

> Sharing the process of generating ideas and discussing the social and emotional elements of writing as a writer-teacher is better suited to contexts where a teacher writes alongside a small group, in such situations, conversations about one's text and the art of writing may emerge more naturally. (2010: 27)

We would certainly encourage anyone engaging in shared writing with children to test their techniques with small groups before working with a whole class, so that confidence in methodology can be developed without the challenges of managing a large group while possibly feeling vulnerable and lacking in confidence in the writing pedagogy. However we approach writing for children, there are some clear benefits, which we describe below.

- It shows that you value writing.
- It models and develops writing strategies.

- It helps you to understand the challenges children face.
- It gives you the opportunity to see how an audience responds to writing.
- It provides a model for children's writing.
- You can target children's interests and even include them in a story.

Research focus: Modelling composition strategies

The Education Endowment Foundation found from meta-analyses of research that 'there is extensive evidence for the impact of teaching writing composition strategies' (EEF, 2017: 15). Its report concluded that writing was a process made up of seven components, which children should be taught to use together with strategies that 'should be carefully modelled and practised' (2017: 14) so that children could gradually assume responsibility for using them independently.

Strategies for writing

The EEF's seven strategies are described below with examples. It is important to emphasise that published authors use similar strategies and that the strategies represent good, established practice.

Planning

Before writing begins ideas need to be discussed and goals set. For example, the purpose of the writing needs to be identified: who is going to read it? What features do I intend to include? The goals or aims can be written down and referred to as the writing develops.

Drafting

An important stage of writing involves drafting. This might include using charts, graphic organisers, notes, bullet points or other types of list. At this stage handwriting, spelling and grammar are not the main focus, but it will be important to organise ideas.

Sharing

Writing can be improved considerably when ideas are shared and discussed with others, including both pupils and teachers. Children might try their ideas out orally and get feedback and advice, or they could swap notes and read each other's ideas. Sharing can take place throughout all stages of writing and can include a focus on spelling, punctuation and grammar at an appropriate stage.

Evaluating

As writing develops, children can check that they are achieving their goals by re-reading and by sharing their text with others. Specific questions might be provided related to the type of writing they are engaged in. For a story these might include:

- Have I varied vocabulary to keep my writing interesting, for example by using variations on 'said' in dialogue, and a range of adjectives and adverbs?
- Is the vocabulary appropriate for my intended readership?
- Have I used sufficient description to help the reader understand the setting?

Revising

Real authors revise their work constantly, both following feedback from others and re-reading themselves. Real writers cross out and amend text so that it sometimes looks messy, if they are writing by hand. Similarly, even when writing is done digitally, tracked changes and comments from others can make presentation untidy, but this is part of the process which leads towards greater accuracy and better-quality writing. Teachers can model posing questions about writing such as:

- How could this be improved?
- Is some of the vocabulary and phrasing repetitive?
- Which synonyms could be used?
- What do you like/dislike?
- Could metaphors or similes be added?
- Is there too much description and not enough action?

Editing

As writers begin to complete their work, it is important that there is a strong focus on accuracy in transcription as well as quality of composition. At this stage it is important to emphasise that correct spelling, punctuation and grammar is vital if readers are to understand the text and engage with its content rather than being distracted by errors in its presentation. Dictionaries, thesauruses and, where appropriate, reference sources to check for factual accuracy can be used, both in hard copy and online at this stage.

Publishing

The final stage is to 'publish' writing so that it can be read by others. Publication might take various forms, from actual public publication (which was the outcome for *Twins?* and *The Wishroom*) to sharing writing in a variety of ways, for example:

- Writing might be displayed in the classroom or elsewhere in the school.
- A book could be printed and bound in-house, or by an online firm such as doxdirect.com.
- Copies could be sent home for family members to read.
- A class book could be created, for example a poetry anthology.
- Stories could be shared with other classes, for example KS2 children writing for KS1 children.

The EEF report advocates using the *gradual release of responsibility model* to teach the strategies. This involves modelling and working with children while giving them increasing autonomy and independence.

> Teachers should introduce each strategy by describing how and when to use it. Then strategies should be modelled. Shared writing allows teachers to 'think-aloud' and share their thought process for each strategy with pupils. (EEF, 2017: 14)

Case study: Writing with one or two children

As part of their English course, primary PGCE trainee teachers at Durham University have some of their lectures in a local school. The lecture is followed immediately by an opportunity to put theory into practice by working with one or two children. One of the themes is writing, and trainees write with and for children and work towards a finished product which they take away, type and incorporate illustrations and present to the children at the next session. The themes and text types are discussed with the children and are determined by the children. Often these are stories, but children also choose to write about their experiences and hobbies. In a second session, the following week, the theme is non-fiction. Children and trainees agree upon topics and find out interesting information between sessions and bring this to the next session. The guidance to the trainees is described below:

- You act as the scribe initially and draw upon the children's ideas.
- Think aloud and demonstrate and discuss aspects such as:
    - Vocabulary choices
    - Different ways to phrase
    - Synonyms
    - Similes
    - Metaphors
    - Layout
- Ask for ideas – although you are scribing, you need to give children 'ownership' of the text.
- Talk about phrasing and spelling.
- Regularly read back what has been written and ask for ideas.

- Change the text if necessary – crossing out is good! It models how real writers write.
- Build the text and get the children writing as well – this might be a sentence or a page – it depends on your child's ability.
- Discuss what the child has written.
- Begin with content, but do discuss spelling and grammar.
- Use lots of praise and encouragement.
- Your child or children may wish to take over scribing or may prefer to let you do the writing using their ideas. Whatever you do, it's important to ensure that the text is theirs and not just yours.
- Resolve differences/conflicts by saying, 'Okay, if you can't agree, each write your own version and then share with others'.
- Share the text with another pair/group and ask for feedback.
- When your children are happy with the final version, take it away and 'publish' it.

One of the highlights of the English course for many trainees is seeing children's reaction when they bring in beautifully presented versions of the children's writing. Often these are laminated or made into booklets with illustrations incorporated. The children's work has, in effect, been published and made available for others to see. Examples can be found in chapter 6 of Jolliffe and Waugh (2018). Of course, as a class teacher with perhaps 30 pupils to manage, you may find it difficult to devote time to individuals and pairs of children in the way described above, but there may be opportunities to work in this way involving well-briefed teaching assistants or when teaching assistants take responsibility for the rest of the class.

In the following sections, we will look at the types of text which you might write with and for children, and at some examples of children's literature which might be starting points or stimuli for writing.

Children's literature as a stimulus for writing

What types of text could you and your class write?

Retelling established stories

This can involve discussion and even drama as a prelude to writing. You might use traditional tales such as Little Red Riding Hood or Goldilocks and the Three Bears as stimuli and then retell the stories orally before writing them with children. Variations can be introduced from children's suggestions, and you might wish to read some alternative versions such as those in Roald Dahl's *Revolting Rhymes* or some of the other collections of retellings. We may think fairy tales are most suitable for younger children, but many have dark and adult themes in their pre-twentieth-century origins, some of which might be studied by older children. To find out more about the origins of fairy tales, try Jessica Doyle's (2021) feature on the *Abe Books* website, but note that some of the origins are particularly gruesome and you may not wish to direct children to the website.

Mini sagas

A development of the fairy tale then could be to attempt to retell established stories in exactly fifty words. Not only does this lead to lots of discussion about what the key events are in a story, but it also raises awareness of language use and the need to be concise without missing key elements of a tale.

Pictures

Books which are told purely though illustrations give scope for imaginative story-telling and discussion. Many schools use the 14 Harris Burdick illustrations as starting points for writing. These beautifully presented black and white drawings each have a title and a caption, but nothing more. There is a fascinating, if possibly apocryphal, story behind the origins of the sketches, which can be found online with an introduction by Lemony Snicket at the *Houghton Mifflin Books* website (Snicket, 2011).

Another way to use illustrations as the foundation for both oral story-telling and writing is to cover text or photograph pictures so that, having read a story, children only have the pictures to help them to retell it. This encourages engagement with and interpretation of pictures. Arizipe and Styles (2016: 180) concluded that the use of well-crafted picture books had 'the potential to "teach" readers both literary and literacy skills as the reader/viewer is encouraged to engage deeply and this can lead to critical thinking and meaningful learning'.

There is an abundance of high quality books available, but one with which we have enjoyed particular success is *The Tunnel* by Anthony Browne: an excellent example of beautiful illustrations carrying meanings which can generate discussion and writing.

Story openings

Make a collection of story openings and ask children to contribute suggestions. Ask them about the story openings which have made them want to read on as well as those which put them off continuing. Discuss different styles of opening from 'Once upon a time …' to those which 'start with a bang' and then gradually fill in information about characters, events and settings. Look at the opening lines of four of the most popular children's novels and consider how you might discuss them with a class:

> Once there were four children whose names were Peter, Susan, Edmund and Lucy. This story is about something that happened to them when they were sent away from London during the war because of the air-raids.
>
> – C.S. Lewis, *The Lion, the Witch and the Wardrobe*

> I disappeared on the night before my twelfth birthday, July 28 1988. Only now can I at last tell the whole extraordinary story, the true story.
>
> – Michael Morpurgo, *Kensuke's Kingdom*

> 'Yes,' said Tom bluntly, on opening the front door. 'What do you want?'
>
> – Michelle Magorian *Goodnight Mr Tom*

> 'Where's Pa going with that axe?' said Fern to her mother as they were setting the table for breakfast.
>
> – E.B. White, *Charlotte's Web*

Explain that you are going to need their help to write a story opening and invite suggestions. Encourage children to look at a range of story openings and to discuss them and rate how likely they would be to want to read on after reading them.

Dialogue

Dialogue in stories enables authors to give insights into characters' personalities while providing a break from continuous prose. The use of different verbs and adverbs offers clues as to how characters speak and punctuation marks such as question and exclamation marks offer further insights. Dialogue can be used to involve children in reading a story if they are assigned roles whereby they read their character's lines while the teacher or another child reads the rest of the text. Not only does this get them to consider how lines should be delivered, but it also makes them more aware of the punctuation of direct speech.

When it comes to writing dialogue with children, there are several possibilities:

- Replicate the style of a book they are currently reading together. For example, using apostrophes to show that a character drops aitches as Roald Dahl does when Sergeant Samways is speaking in *Danny the Champion of the World*, or using non-standard subject verb correspondences like 'I is' and invented words such as *crockadowndillies* and *horrigust* when the *BFG* talks.
- Dramatising and then writing dialogue between characters in situations which they predict may arise as a story progresses can challenge children to think about character traits. They can play parts and take part in

conversations before writing direct speech or a short script to share with others, who can be asked to read it in role.

- Learning how to present and punctuate dialogue can be incorporated into creative activities. Besides focusing on punctuation, this can explore limiting use of *said* and finding a range of verbs which convey how characters speak. There can also be opportunities to look at a range of adverbs to accompany the verbs.
- Interesting examples of dialogue from children's literature can be displayed and be a topic for discussion, as well as being examples of what might be possible in children's independent writing.

Poetry

Before considering how we might write poetry with children, it is worth considering some of the challenges which poetry presents, given the many different types of poem.

Research focus: Poetry writing and modelling literary forms

Anthony Wilson (2007), a published poet and primary educator, found that there were both benefits and drawbacks to modelling literary forms for children. He argued that the benefits could be temporary, firstly because poetry requires children 'to unlearn rules learnt in prose writing', and secondly because there are many different poetic forms. So when children have mastered, say, haiku or acrostics, they then need to acquire an understanding of other formats such as limericks, cinquains, triolets and tankas.

As Wilson maintains: 'poetry writing requires children to be flexible thinkers because every time they work within a different form, or from a different literary model, they are unlearning the "rules" of other poetic forms' (2007: 453–454).

He argues that 'literary forms may only have limited use for developing knowledge transformation skills, unless the modeling and knowledge of the teacher concerned is of a high order' (2007: 454).

Appreciating the qualities of poetry and being able to write and perform it clearly makes demands upon both teachers and pupils. However, in a curriculum which is laden with terminology for children to use and understand, it might be argued that poetry can enable them to become familiar with this vocabulary in a meaningful way. Primary teacher Nigel Clements worked with his class to film them performing poetry and this led to public presentations which engaged both the children and their audiences. An interesting observation was that 'One enormous advantage of this activity was that it enabled me to make explicit some "knowledge about language" in a meaningful context'. Clements cited examples, including 'verse, blank verse, rhyme, rhythm, imagery, mood, tone, alliteration, similes, metaphors, style, verbs, adverbs, and adjectives'. He noted too that there was also 'a considerable amount of terminology that related to aspects of performance: intonation, expression, pace, clarity, diction, dramatic pauses, light and shade, voices' (Clements, 1994: 21)

In Chapter 8, we explored poetry in greater depth, but when it comes to writing poetry with children, there are some things we can do to make the activity less challenging.

Read and share examples

Whatever kind of poetry you and the children write, begin by sharing examples and talking about structure and language features. For example, for haiku, children need to see that this very short format can enable poets to express something quite profound or pithy in very few words. They also need to be able to count syllables and apply this to words so that they get the structure right. After reading examples and discussing them, it's a good idea to model writing some, drawing on children's ideas and discussing how words might be replaced if they don't fit with the syllable count. Once children have experienced haiku, you might wish to share other poetry where syllables need to be counted such as tankas and limericks, and you can begin to look at scansion in a range of poetry.

Create word banks for rhymes

If the poetry you and your class write is to rhyme, it is essential that the children have access to a range of appropriate rhyming vocabulary. This can be created with children's help by inviting them to suggest words which might feature in the theme for a poem and then asking for suggestions for words which rhyme. This can lead to discussions about phonemes and spelling, but crucially it will help avoid trite and meaningless rhymes and will broaden children's lexicons.

Films and recordings of poems

As Clements' work described in the case study above illustrates, there can be benefits from sharing poetry through filming. The poetry children write independently and with our help might also be recorded as film or using a voice recorder.

Maps and stories

A map is a great accompaniment to a story. So many children's classics have maps, often as the end-papers to the book. From the Hundred Acre Wood to

Middle Earth, from Narnia via the river of The Wind in the Willows to the lake of Swallows and Amazons, a map can be a wonderful way to make a story real to the reader. You can look at the map before reading, to guess at events and narrative, consult it during the reading, and trace the story afterwards by looking at it. So, when writing with children, drawing a map together to show the framework for the story can be a helpful exercise, as well as being fun, creative and an arresting centrepiece for the story's eventual display.

Predictions

At the end of an episode of a story, ask children to predict what might happen next. For younger children, write their suggestions down and display or share them before the next episode. Older children might record their predictions in a notebook or on Post-its, which can be attached to a display board related to the book.

Replicating style

Roger Hargreaves' Little Miss or Mr Men books are short and humorous and have characters who are easy to draw. Create your own Little Miss or Mr Men books, either using existing characters or inventing new ones. These could be started off with an example being produced through shared writing, before children go on to work in groups. Encourage children to read several of the books so that they become familiar with the style and can attempt to replicate it.

Food as a stimulus

Nearly all children like food. Descriptions of food and meals are a sure-fire winner: think of Enid Blyton's Famous Five stories and what you remember are the delicious farmhouse teas, the picnics and, of course, the lashings of ginger beer! You might remember Alice's drink tasting of 'a mixed flavour of cherry-tart, custard, pineapple, roast turkey, toffee and hot buttered toast', Lucy's tea with Mr Tumnus ('a nice brown egg … sardines on toast, then buttered toast, then toast with honey, and then a sugar-topped cake') or the Water Rat's picnic of 'cold chicken … cold tongue cold ham cold beef pickled gherkins salad French rolls potted meat ginger beer lemonade soda water …'. Describing a favourite meal – the look, the smells, the sensations of eating – is a good way to get your class talking, comparing and writing. The following websites provide lots of ideas:

Moore, B. (2019) *Children's Books About Food*. Available at: https://www.thespruceeats.com/childrens-books-about-food-1665921 (accessed 12 November 2021).

Children's Fiction Cooking Food Books. Available at:

https://www.alibris.co.uk/search/books/subject/Children%27s-Fiction-Cooking-Food?qsort=&page=5&matches=2518 (accessed 12 November 2021).

The theme of healthy eating can be addressed and discussed through engaging children with stories and poems. For younger children, *Bread and Jam for Frances* by Russell Hoban tells the story of Frances who only wants to eat her favourite food – bread and jam. However, when Frances's mother agrees to only serve her bread and jam, she starts to look with more interest at what the rest of her family and friends are eating and soon wants to enjoy more variety.

Journeys

Have you ever noticed how many books start with a journey? Often the protagonist is on a train, or in a car or a cart, depending on how old the book is, looking out of the window and wondering about the adventures awaiting at the end of it. You may have read *Carrie's War* (Nina Bawden), *Five Children and It* (E. Nesbit), *The Children of Green Knowe* (Lucy Boston) or many others. It's a good starting point, firstly because it is so obviously the beginning of a new episode in the character's life, secondly because it gives the reader a chance to meet the person in isolation before the story begins, thirdly because we can share the anticipation and excitement of the unknown ahead. Try giving an open start like, 'Kim was staring out of the window at the unfamiliar landscape they were passing through …' and see where it takes them!

An extension of the idea of journeys is, of course, the magical journeys which take one to other worlds. Finding a whole new world inside a cuckoo clock, at the back of a wardrobe, under the bed or through a strange tollbooth which appears in your bedroom, gives scope for as much fantasy and imagination as your writers want.

Publishing

In this chapter, we have explored a range of stimuli for writing with children. When we write and discuss reading and writing we learn about language, including learning about language features incidentally. As we have seen, children can also learn about publication and the strategies authors use as they refine and complete their work. We conclude with a look at some of the ways in which writing can be 'published' so that there is a real 'audience' for it.

Wall displays

The traditional way of publishing work is to display it attractively on classroom and corridor walls. This can encourage careful proof-reading and close attention to handwriting, but if lengthy pieces of writing are produced, it can be a tedious task for children to copy or type them out. It can, therefore, be a good idea to ask them to choose a favourite section such as an opening, some dialogue or an exciting description to hone and refine for display.

Presentations

These might be PowerPoint slides with writing accompanied by pictures imported from online sources or could involve children reading and even dramatising their writing for classmates or in an assembly. The advantage of the PowerPoint and similar media is that there is a permanent recording which can be shared over and again, but performing in front of a live audience can be a valuable way of developing children's confidence and awareness of the need to communicate effectively. As the National Curriculum states, children should be able to 'write clearly, accurately and coherently, adapting their language and style in and for a range of contexts, purposes and audiences' (DfE, 2013: 13).

Recordings

Writing can also be recorded using voice recorders and by filming. Again, there can be a permanent record which can be shared widely. Children can re-record when they make mistakes or simply want to improve presentation. They can also be shown examples of professional recordings of stories and poems to give them ideas for their own.

Anthologies

Collections of stories and poems can be produced using a range of self-publishing methods. These might be printed and copies made for children and their families.

Websites

Finally, all schools now have websites and these can include sections where writing examples are shared and available for families to view. Caution should be exercised to ensure that individual children whose writing is below the expected level are not exposed. Indeed, it may be wise to use websites only to share writing which is produced collectively.

However you decide to publish the writing produced by you and your class, keep in mind the importance of valuing writing and celebrating quality. Make yourself familiar with a range of children's literature, including poetry, so that you can provide examples of different genres and alert children to texts they can enjoy and can draw upon for ideas and inspiration.

Learning outcomes review

By reading this chapter, you will have considered:

- The importance of creating children's literature with children
- How teachers can develop children's understanding of and engagement with texts
- The value of stories and some simple ways of engaging children in writing them
- A range of possible writing activities
- Ways of 'publishing' children's writing

Questions for discussion

- How confident do you feel about modelling writing for children?
- Are you familiar with techniques for shared writing?
- Are you familiar with a range of text genres and confident about explaining them?

For your bookshelf

Bawden, N. (1973) *Carrie's War.* London: Puffin.
Eleven-year-old Carrie and her brother are evacuated to Wales during the Second World War, and have to learn about relationships between the adults they are living among.

Blyton, Enid. *The Famous Five* (there are 21 books about the Famous Five).
Easy to read, dramatic adventures which have been perennially popular and helped establish reading 'chapter books' as a habit for generations.

Boston, L.M. (1954) *The Children of Green Knowe.* London: Faber & Faber.
First in a series of books in which Tolly learns about the history of his grandmother's house through the ghosts of children who have lived there over the centuries.

Browne, A. (1989) *The Tunnel.* London: Julia MacRae. PowerPoint available at https://in.pinterest.com/pin/176203404152110611/ (accessed 12 November 2021).
A wordless adventure for the readers to supply their own narrative, which can be an insight into relationships between brother and sister.

Dahl, R. (1975) *Danny the Champion of the World.* London: Jonathan Cape.
Danny's father teaches him the secrets of poaching pheasants, in an exciting story told with detail and humour.

Grahame, K. (1908) *The Wind in the Willows*. London: Methuen.
The classic of country life, with the humour of Toad's adventures mixed with evocative passages describing the everyday life of the river bank.

Hargreaves, Roger. *The Mr Men* and *Little Miss* series.
Simple and short, with clear lessons to be learnt from every character, these are a good stimulus for children to produce their own stories.

Hoban, R. (1964) *Bread and Jam for Frances*. London: Harper & Row (and others).
For younger children, the illustrated adventures of the little badger Frances as she learns to try new food, share with a baby sister, or stay in bed when she's told to, are funny and delightful.

Lewis, C.S. (1950) *The Lion, the Witch and the Wardrobe*. London: Geoffrey Bles.
The first of the Chronicles of Narnia, this story combines magic and adventure as four children find a whole unknown world full of enchantment.

Magorian, M. (1981) *Goodnight Mr Tom*. London: Kestrel Books.
An evacuee leaves his deprived childhood in London to find a whole new life in the countryside. Some adult themes make this a book better approached with Year 5/6.

Morpurgo, M. (1999) *Kensuke's Kingdom*. London: Egmont.
Everyone has imagined, surely, being shipwrecked on a desert island? But in this story it turns out not to be quite deserted ... descriptive and practical details make the book a real page-turner.

Nesbit, E. (1902) *Five Children and It*. London: T. Fisher Unwin.
Nesbit's wonderful and timeless evocations of family relationships are at their best in her magic stories – the Sand Fairy grants wishes but somehow they always go wrong.

Ransome, A. (1930) *Swallows and Amazons*. London: Jonathan Cape.
The timeless stories of children sailing in the Lake District, whose adventures and deeds are always enhanced by their imaginations.

Rowling, J.K. (1997) *Harry Potter and the Philosopher's Stone*. London: Bloomsbury.
The first in the series – school story, magic and the start of an epic quest all in one!

Webb, K. and Maitland, A. (2016) *I like this Poem*. London: Puffin.
A comprehensive anthology of all kinds of poetry, from funny to thought-provoking to tragic, chosen by children as their favourites.

White, E.B. (1952) *Charlotte's Web*. London: Hamish Hamilton.
A must for animal-lovers, as the brave and clever spider Charlotte constantly comes up with ideas to save piglet Wilbur's bacon.

Further reading

To find out more about how *The Wishroom* was created, see Waugh, D. (2019) Writing with children, in A. Bushnell, R. Smith and D. Waugh, *Modelling Exciting Writing*. London: Sage (pp. 46–61).

You can find out more about the project in Waugh, D. (2018) Talk, reading comprehension and writing, in D. Jones and P. Hodson, *Unlocking Speaking and Listening*, 3rd edition. London: David Fulton.

For ideas for writing and lesson plans, see Bushnell, A., Smith, R. and Waugh, D. (2020) *100 Ideas for Primary Teachers: Writing*. London: Bloomsbury.

For ideas and a rationale for visual literacy, see the Literacy Ideas for Teachers and Students website:

https://www.literacyideas.com/teaching-visual-texts-in-the-classroom/ (accessed 12 November 2021).

For a range of practical ideas for poetry, see Sandy Brownjohn's excellent books:

Brownjohn, S. (1980) *Does It Have to Rhyme?* London: Hodder Education.
Brownjohn, S. (1982) *What Rhymes with Secret?* London: Hodder Education.
Brownjohn, S. (1989) *The Ability to Name Cats*. London: Hodder Education.

References

Anderson, H. (2020) Surprising secrets of writers' first book drafts, *BBC Culture*, 19 August. Available at: https://www.bbc.com/culture/article/20200818-surprising-secrets-of-writers-first-book-drafts (accessed 18 February 2022).

Arizipe, E. and Styles, M. (2016) *Children Reading Picturebooks: Interpreting Visual Texts*, 2nd edition. London: Routledge.

Baker, S. and Cremin, T. (2018) Teachers' identities as writers, in T. Cremin and T. Locke (eds.) *Writer Identity and the Teaching and Learning of Writing*. London: Routledge (pp. 98–114).

Clements, N. (1994) *Poetry on the Pulse*. UKRA Reading. Oxford: Blackwell.

Cremin, T. and Baker, S. (2010) Exploring teacher-writer identities in the classroom: Conceptualising the struggle, *English Teaching: Practice and Critique*, 9 (3): 8–25.

Department for Education (DfE) (2011) *Teachers' Standards: Guidance for school leaders, school staff and governing bodies* (updated 2013 and 2021). London: DfE. Available at: https://www.gov.uk/government/publications/teachers-standards (accessed 16 February 2022).

Department for Education (DfE) (2013) *The National Curriculum in England: Key Stages 1 and 2 Framework Document*. Available at: https://www.gov.uk/government/publications/national-curriculum-in-england-primary-curriculum (accessed 3 September 2021).

Doyle, J. (2021) *The gruesome origins of classic fairy tales*. Available at: https://www.abebooks.com/books/the-gruesome-origins-of-classic-fairy-tales/ (accessed 16 February 2022).

Durham Commission on Creativity and Education (2019) Arts Council England and Durham University. Available at: https://www.dur.ac.uk/creativitycommission/ (accessed 18 February 2022).

Education Endowment Foundation (EEF) (2017) *Improving Literacy in Key Stage 2: Guidance report*. London: EEF. Available at: https://files.eric.ed.gov/fulltext/ED612216.pdf (accessed 18 February 2022).

Elisondo, R. (2016) Creativity is always a social process, *Creativity: Theories, Research, Applications*, 3 (2): 194–210.

Falconer, E., Cropley, D. and Dollard, M. (2018) An exploration of creativity in primary school children, *International Journal of Creativity and Problem-Solving*, 28 (2): 7–25.

Hughes, D. (2020) Deeper writing through writing for children, in A. Bushnell, A. Gill and D. Waugh (eds.) *Mastering Writing at Greater Depth*. London: Sage.

Jolliffe, W. and Waugh, D. (2018) *Mastering Primary English*. London: Bloomsbury.

Kampylis, P. and Berki, E. (2014) *Nurturing Creative Thinking*. Educational Practices Series #25. Brussels: International Academy of Education. Available at: https://unesdoc.unesco.org/ark:/48223/pf0000227680 (accessed 12 November 2021).

Knight, S. and Mercer, N. (2015) The role of exploratory talk in classroom search engine tasks, *Technology, Pedagogy and Education*, 24 (3): 303–319.

Snicket, L. (2011) *Who is Harris Burdock?* Available at: http://www.houghtonmifflinbooks.com/features/harrisburdick/ (accessed 12 November 2021).

Waugh, D. (2016) *Jessica's Other World*. YouCaxton Publications.

Waugh, D., Sanderson, R., McMahon, E., Stewart, I., Kay, A., Joyce, F., Armstrong, G., Hood, A., Martin, E., Wood, T., Gibbins, I., Atkinson, I., English, B., Appleby, S., Halsall, F., Pearson, A., Harris, A., Dawson, G., Fisher, A., Waistell, R., Semple, K., Hird, E., Fortune, H., Boxall, L., Swan-Learoyd-Ashmain, S., Watkins, E., Ramage, L., Mawson, L., Frater, C., Rutter-Bryson, H., Gilling, P., Robinson, C., Elves, J., Humphries, A., Robson, N., Wilson, B., Moore, D., Myers, A., Blair, T., Dawson, B., Crane, D., Nicholson, A., Cooper, V., Watt, P., Colles, M., Pierce, J., Piercy, H. and& Taylor, G. (2017) *The Wishroom*. Bishop's Castle: Constance Books.

Waugh, D., Anderson, L., Castling, J., Cross, C., Dixon, K., Fernandes, R., Goldsborough, E., Henderson, C., Hutton, C., Maddison, M., Richardson, A., Stubbs, E., Wallace, A. and Jarvis, H. (2019) *Twins?*. Bishop's Castle: Constance Books.

Wilson, A. (2007) Finding a voice? Do literary forms work creatively in teaching poetry writing?, *Cambridge Journal of Education*, 37 (3): 441–457.

Conclusion: What next?

> *"Teachers need to have wide and deep repertoires of children's literature and get to know the interests and practices of the young readers in their classes."*
>
> – Cremin, 2021: 7

We hope you have enjoyed our book and that you will consider using some of the ideas we have suggested and those of the many teachers who have contributed case studies or told us about their good practice. We know, from our many years as educators, that children's literature can not only be enjoyed for the intrinsic pleasure it gives, but also enhances teaching and learning across the curriculum.

We know, too, both from our experience and the research by people like Teresa Cremin, the importance of teachers knowing a range of texts and being able to draw on these to guide, enrich and support children's reading. This knowledge enables us to select texts which can enhance work across the curriculum, as well as providing us with a bank of ideas for stories and poems which might engage and enthuse our pupils.

Having said that, one of the pleasures of writing this book has been the wealth of new material we have found, on bookshelves, online and in conversations. In teaching, it is always important to keep up with new developments and new ways to enjoy reading: there is always more to learn. Keep reading as a high-profile element in your classroom. Your classes can introduce you to writers and stories they love; from conversations with children, you can find out what they enjoy, the topics they like to feature in stories and poems, and the authors whose work they read most. And you, of course, can use your own repertoire to recommend books to them on an individual level.

Talk with colleagues about the strategies they use to integrate children's literature into the curriculum and try to be part of a 'teachers as readers' culture in your school and perhaps beyond. Look at your classroom and school and consider whether there is an environment which is conducive to celebrating children's literature and children's engagement with it.

You might also try writing with and for children, as suggested in our final chapter, so that they see that stories and poems are not the preserve of published authors, but can be created, shared and enjoyed by people like you and them.

Above all, keep reading! Be open to trying texts which are recommended by colleagues, websites and children. Don't fall into the trap of thinking that children's literature is only to be read by children – or, indeed, that all adult literature is exclusively for grown-ups. Our house is full of children's literature, all of it well-thumbed and read. It's never too late to start your own collection and if you do, you may find that your teaching and children's learning across the curriculum is embellished.

Reference

Cremin, T. (2021) Building communities of engaged readers, in A. Gill, M. Stephenson and D. Waugh (eds.) *Developing a Love of Reading and Books*. London: Learning Matters.

Index